GATHERINGS
America's Quilt Heritage

Gatherings

America's Quilt Heritage

a project of the Museum of the American Quilter's Society
funded in part by a grant from the Lila Wallace-Reader's Digest Fund

Text by Kathlyn F. Sullivan
based on information gathered from state quilt documentation projects,
other interviews, and correspondence.

Developed in conjunction with an exhibit curated by
Paul D. Pilgrim and Gerald E. Roy

Appendices by Katy Christopherson

American Quilter's Society
P. O. Box 3290 • Paducah, KY 42002-3290

Library of Congress Cataloging-in-Publication Data

Sullivan, Kathlyn F.
    Gatherings: America's quilt heritage / Kathlyn F. Sullivan ; appendices by Katy Christopherson ; curated by Paul Pilgrim & Gerald Roy.
    p.   cm.
    Published on the occasion of an exhibition held at the Museum of the American Quilters' Society of quilts chosen by state quilt heritage documentation projects.
    Includes bibliographical references (p.) and indexes.
    ISBN 0-89145-860-3 : $34.95
    1. Quilts--United States--History--Exhibitions.   2. Quiltmakers--United States--Exhibitions.   3. Quilts--Collectors and collection--United States--Exhibitions.   I. Christopherson, Katy.   II. Roy, Gerald E.   III. Pilgrim, Paul D.   IV. MAQS.   V. Title.
NK9112.S86   1995
746.46'00973'07476995--dc20
                                                                                                                   95--9952
                                                                                                                                           CIP

Additional copies of this book may be ordered from:

American Quilter's Society
P.O. Box 3290
Paducah, KY 42002-3290
@34.95. Add $1.00 for postage and handling.

Copyright: 1995, Museum of the American Quilter's Society

This book or any part thereof may not be reproduced without the written consent of the Museum of the American Quilter's Society and Publisher.

Printed by IMAGE GRAPHICS, INC., Paducah, Kentucky

Dedication

Dedicated to those of the present
who both conserve the past and create the future: volunteers all, willingly sharing their quilts,
their time, their knowledge, their resources,
and especially their hearts.

Exhibit Schedule

Museum of the American Quilter's Society
Paducah, KY
April 15 – August 12, 1995

Portions of the exhibit will travel in 1995–1996 to

New England Quilt Museum
Lowell, MA

Monmouth Museum
Lincroft, NJ

Colorado Springs Pioneers Museum
Colorado Springs, CO

Kentucky Museum, Western Kentucky University
Bowling Green, KY

For a complete schedule write:
MAQS
PO Box 1540

Acknowledgments

"GATHERINGS: America's Quilt Heritage" has been made possible in part by a grant from the Lila Wallace-Reader's Digest Fund. Additional support has come from individuals, corporations, quilt guilds, and Friends of MAQS. The Gatherings Celebration Weekend, April 21–23, 1995, is made possible by support from Benartex, Inc., and publication of this book is made possible by the American Quilter's Soctiety (AQS).

The Museum of the American Quilter's Society (MAQS) extends special thanks to book author Kathlyn F. Sullivan, exhibit curators Paul D. Pilgrim and Gerald E. Roy, and other advisory board members – Katy Christopherson, chair, Cuesta Benberry, Victoria Faoro, Sandi Fox, Meredith Schroeder, and Helen Thompson – who have given many hours and much expertise over the past four years to make this book, and the exhibit and videotape possible.

Special thanks also goes to the many individuals who have served as contacts for their states for quilt selection and loans, and also reported and checked the data. Without them, this book would not have been possible.

Each quilt owner, whether an individual or institution, has contributed not just a textile treasure, but also valuable photos and documents, along with many hours spent sharing with us information about the quiltmakers and their lives. These stories and the wonderful quilts with which they are connected are the heart of this publication and the exhibit it accompanies.

And, of course, we would not have had any of these wonderful resources available here were it not for the countless volunteer hours spent making each state documentation project a reality.

MAQS is grateful for the efforts that all have contributed.

Foreword

Bruce Mann of Louisville, Kentucky, started it all, when he proposed that the quilts of Kentucky should be documented.

As for GATHERINGS, it was a simple idea, "There ought to be an exhibition of quilts from all the projects." But who was free to do it? Paul Pilgrim and Gerald Roy were suggested. Confronted with the concept they responded immediately, and planning began in the spring of 1991. It was Paul and Jerry who proposed that an added dimension was needed, namely that GATHERINGS should celebrate the volunteers, as well as the quilts and their makers.

The curators, the author, the Advisory Committee, and the staff of the Museum of the American Quilter's Society present this book, and the exhibition it accompanies, as a tribute to all those volunteers who have so willingly devoted time to the state quilt projects and without whom these projects could not have been done.

Katy Christopherson
January 1995

Table of Contents

Preface by Paul D. Pilgrim and Gerald R. Roy, exhibit curators 10
Introduction by Kathlyn F. Sullivan, book author 12

Chapter 1 13
The Quilt Heritage Documentaion Projects:
The Need to Know, Preserve, and Celebrate

Chapter 2 21
Quilt Documentation Days:
Sharing, Exploring, and Imaging

Chapter 3 47
Quilts and Their Makers:
Infinite Varieties

Chapter 4 147
Quilt Owners:
Custodians of the Heritage

Chapter 5 173
The Discoveries Continue:
Interactions and Results Greater Than the Sum of Their Parts

Appendices 206
State Quilt Projects 207
State Contacts 216
Endnotes 218
Bibliography 219
Index 221

Preface

It does not seem strange to us that quilts occupy most of our time and have for the past 26 years. It *does* come as a constant surprise that many people know little about these textile treasures. We have been fortunate to be able to turn what began as involvement in a quilt business into a life of collecting, teaching, curating, writing, and working with quilts in other ways that help make people aware of their value as family history and material culture.

The important contributions to public education about quilts made by individual state quilt documentation projects became very obvious to us as we began reading the books these organizations published. The accomplishments of each project were astonishing; not having been involved personally, we marveled at them, and wondered exactly how such undertakings could be completed. The logistics would be astounding, as would be the expense. The state documentation project phenomenon fascinated us, so when Katy Christopherson approached us with her idea of our curating an exhibition displaying quilts from each state, we imagined this might be our opportunity to explore such questions for ourselves and for others.

Wanting this effort to be more than a quilt exhibition, we were determined that the results celebrate the efforts of the many volunteers who made state projects possible. The title "GATHERINGS: America's Quilt Heritage" evolved as the original planning committee met to discuss the exhibit and related activities. It was determined GATHERINGS would solicit information and quilt nominations from each state representative. We encouraged states to nominate quilts that had not already been included in state publications. Rather than looking for the most outstanding artistic examples, state representatives were encouraged to look for quilts strongly linked with people, quilts with fascinating stories involving volunteers or discovered by the largely volunteer-run documentation process. Hopefully GATHERINGS has provided an opportunity for states to bring attention to some unsung heroines and heroes.

Through information collected from state projects, GATHERINGS would also present a comprehensive picture of the volunteer phenomenon that allowed the documentation projects to function, as well as give accurate, up-to-date data on activity and accomplishments. Ultimately our objective has been to direct attention to and generate an appreciation for all the effort put forth by the thousands of volunteers who have taken part in this enormous task. We also hoped that GATHERINGS might offer enough information and encouragement that remaining states might be inspired to conduct their own searches. From the earliest conception to what has finally evolved, "GATHERINGS: America's Quilt Heritage" has grown quite naturally. Through the efforts of many people, it has become an exhibition and a book.

GATHERINGS, like quilt collecting and quiltmaking, has provided us with one more avenue of expression. We have been privileged to work with old friends and cultivate new friends and acquaintances while expanding our knowledge and understanding of quilts and their makers. As the state documentation projects owe their success to volunteers, we owe a great deal of thanks to all those who worked over the past four years to make "GATHERINGS: America's Quilt Heritage" a reality. A special thank you goes to all who have generously supported this project.

Paul D. Pilgrim and Gerald E. Roy
Exhibit Curators

Introduction

While "GATHERINGS: America's Quilt Heritage" was developed as an exhibition, I was asked to incorporate the exhibit selections as a basis for a longer lasting tribute to the quilt documentation projects. It has been a pleasurable experience to reread quilt documentation books and peruse exhibition catalogs from across the United States. I recommend to all their visual delight and fascinating historical perspective.

Like the quilt projects themselves, the compilation of material from each project has been a collaborative effort, involving trust and action by many individuals. Most of the information presented here was provided by members of the various projects, individual quilt owners, and institutions lending to the exhibit. The reader can assume these sources. Every effort has been made to ensure accuracy.

Thank you to those who came out of project retirement to respond to the GATHERINGS requests. Special thanks to Paul Pilgrim, Gerald Roy, Katy Christopherson, Helen Thompson, Victoria Faoro, Julie Powell, Mark Sullivan, and New Horizon Quilters for their knowledge and encouragement. Once again, my life has been enriched by recording the heritage of others.

Kathlyn F. Sullivan

Chapter 1

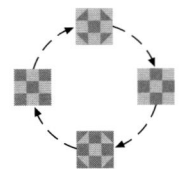

THE QUILT HERITAGE DOCUMENTATION PROJECTS
The Need to Know, Preserve, and Celebrate

This book is a compendium of stories about people and quilts. Both are so intertwined that it is difficult to know where or when the human spirits leave off and the souls of the quilts begin.

Every quilt tells a unique tale and reflects the social and economic context in which it was made. The narrators of these stories are not necessarily just the makers but may also include many others – academics and amateurs, quilt owners and quilt lovers, and those involved with visual arts, textiles, anthropology, folklore, genealogy, women's studies, and history. Many of these stories can be told only because countless individuals from these and other backgrounds joined endeavors that surprised even themselves. Over the past 15 years, regional and statewide groups have spawned what are now referred to as *quilt projects*, organized efforts to record and document the quilts and quiltmakers of a region or state.

"GATHERINGS: America's Quilt Heritage" was conceived by Kentuckian Katy Christopherson, who immediately approached Paul D. Pilgrim and Gerald E. Roy of California about curating the exhibit. Their interest in quilts takes many forms – as quiltmakers; as teachers of design and technique; as collectors, appraisers, curators, and fabric designers.

One aspect of quilt activity that somehow passed them by was participation in a documentation project. But they were very aware of the results of these efforts. When the exhibits and publications appeared, the bodies of material impressed them, and they found the grassroots efforts by vast teams of quilters and quilt lovers overwhelming. They were intrigued by the stories that came to light, by the Herculean volunteer effort itself, and by the resulting positive changes in the quilt owners' attitudes towards their textiles. Bets Ramsey of the Quilts of Tennessee project puts the result of the quilt projects this way: "We've encouraged a sense of family pride, individual accomplishment, and the passing on of traditions."[1] With that in mind, Pilgrim and Roy wanted "GATHERINGS: America's Quilt Heritage" to celebrate the human elements of the documentation projects.

Early quilt scholars like Florence Peto and Dr. William Rush Dunton, Jr. had dealt with American quilts in general; however, before the 1970s there were few bodies of information about specific quilts, their makers, and their geographic areas. With the exception of Amish studies there was little investigation into placing quilts in social and economic contexts. In 1977 Joyce Joines Newman and Mary Ann Emmons, under a Youthgrant from the National Endowment for the Humanities, embarked on a study of quilts from three distinct areas of North Carolina settled by three separate ethnic groups. Their work encompassed that done by Laurel McKay Horton, another folklore student from the University of North Carolina, whose master's thesis had dealt with German and Scotch-Irish elements in quilts from Rowan County (NC). Newman felt that "While published studies of quilting and quilt design argue the existence of a distinctively American quilt design tradition, little attempt has been made to explore regional subtypes or to define distinctive characteristics. A few regional styles have been recognized, but often remain vaguely defined or unsubstantiated."[2] A month-long exhibit was held in 1978 at the Ackland Art Museum on the University of North Carolina campus in Chapel Hill.

The movement towards statewide projects began with Kentucky. A Louisville, Kentucky, antique dealer, Bruce Mann, had been appalled by the number of quilts being bought up and taken from the state, some to be cut into fashions with little concern for their demise and with no regard for their provenance or value as art objects. Mann regarded this as an irreplaceable loss of Kentucky heritage. He proposed a three-part project encompassing the location and documentation of quilts, a resulting museum exhibition, and a book reflecting the findings. The seeds of The Kentucky Quilt Project, Inc. were planted but had yet to grow when Mann's life ended tragically in 1980 as the result of an automobile accident. His friends Eleanor Bingham Miller and Shelly Zegart decided to carry on with the project. They were joined by Eunice Sears and Katy Christopherson.³ Wildly successful and reaching a wide audience, the Kentucky documentation project gave rise to a national phenomenon of recording the history of quilts and quiltmakers.

In spite of the reality that it was too late to record the story of many quilts, the great impetus was the rapid passing of what knowledge remained. Experience showed that quilts get used up and destroyed. Generations pass on and with them the intimate knowledge of their quiltmaking or the stories they'd heard at grandma's knee. Fear of the loss of that knowledge of family, mixed with a regard for the past and a desire for a fraction of immortality, were motivating factors. The quilt documentation "movement" was on. Not undertaken lightly, it was approached with seriousness and some trepidation. Leadership involved a huge commitment. A sense of adventure, a genuine love of quilts, and a great deal of stamina were the primary essentials required. Nebraska Quilt Project director Frankie Best summed it up this way: "As a project director, you need the freedom of an older woman, the endurance of a younger woman, and the tenacity of a hound dog on the trail of a rabbit."⁴

Like the art of quilting, which was passed from one generation to the next, so it went with the quilt projects. Katy Christopherson of Louisville, Kentucky, was a consultant to The Kentucky Quilt Project, Inc. and was indefatigable in bringing those interested together to discuss methodology, forms, computers, and documentation. In 1984, joined by Ricky Clark as co-chair,

she hosted a meeting in Knoxville, Tennessee, taking advantage of the fact that quilt historians from all over the country were in the area for an American Quilt Study Group seminar. Many attendees were already involved in quilt documentation projects or were likely to be in the future. Experts in the fields of computer data entry, research methodology, and other documentation resources were included to help explore and refine data collection methodology. Consistency and thoroughness of collection were of high priority. Development and perfection of the "ultimate" data form received extensive investigation and analysis.

More recent projects have relied on practices developed through the experiences of earlier ones. Nothing teaches like experience, and throughout the United States projects experimented, redesigned, and passed on their knowledge. Quilt experts nationwide were called on to give workshops on fabrics and dating. Seminars and training sessions were held on documentation and methodology. Volunteers participated in trial runs and practice sessions. By the time the Illinois Quilt Research Project began their project in 1988, chairperson Cheryl Kennedy felt that they "owed their beginnings to the Indiana Quilt Research Project as they had not only shared their organizational process but came…and trained us in our own mock quilt day…." She comments further, "Our forms…are what we felt were the best of many. We did not reinvent the wheel and found all project leaders supportive and helpful…"⁵ It should be noted, however, that each project team developed its own unique style and variable goals. Time, money, personnel, space, territory, volunteers, geography, settlement patterns, and priorities are just some of the areas that made each project different yet still part of the whole.

Museum, historical society, and/or university sponsorship proved to be invaluable to various projects. Such affiliation not only gave institutional credibility to the work, but often ensured the use of more stringent methodology. In addition, the use of university students working for academic credit helped bolster the volunteer corps. In many cases, the universities or museums became repositories for all of the gathered information. Some also provided the site and expertise for mounting an exhibit. With the cooperation and advice of those from so many diverse backgrounds, the "exciting by-product of this direction has been the growing seriousness with which the study of quilts is viewed," according to Christopherson. "The impact has begun to be felt far beyond the immediate worlds of the quiltmaker and the quilt historian," she adds.[6]

At the final banquet held in 1991 to celebrate the publication of their project book, *Nebraska Quilts and Quiltmakers,* Nebraska Quilt Project director Frankie Best was overwhelmed when during that "misty-eyed evening," she was presented with a friendship quilt made by members of the project. (Plate 1-1) Each block signified a phase of the experience and reflected the loyalty, dedication, and commitment required to successfully complete a quilt documentation project. The presentation of the quilt was a total surprise.

The members wanted to "make a quilt that would be a record of the experience that they had shared," according to project member, Kari Ronning. After a discussion about their times together, Kari went home and found traditional block patterns that would represent those things. The first block made was Millie Fauquet's original Pine Ridge Star, designed when the group was documenting quilts in the Pine Ridge area of northwestern Nebraska. That, according to Kari, "set the basic fabric choices." Members sewed the top together and it was completed by the quilters of Grace Lutheran Church in Fairbury, Nebraska.

The Snowflake block represents their first scheduled Quilt History Day, subsequently canceled when a late March blizzard hit with fury. The Church block recalls quilt day sites, the Country Roads block reveals the long treks, the Morning Star block tells of the early starts. The Boxes, Telephone, and Envelope blocks reiterate all the arranging and paperwork associated with running quilt days. "You should have seen my dining room," groans the director.

The additional blocks in Frankie's quilt celebrate the collaborative effort and its results with themes like fun, compatibility, and new quilt discoveries. The Orange Peel block was for Frankie's favorite shared snack. The Fan block is a memorial to project member Mary Obrist, who succumbed to breast cancer at age 40 before the project had been completed. Kari explains that, "the last block, Friendship Knot, signifies

Plate 1-1.
Memories of the Nebraska Quilt Project
75" x 91".
1991.
Nebraska Quilt Project Committee.
Made in Lincoln, NE.
Cotton top.
Collection: Frankie Best.
Photo: Richard Walker.
Created in conjunction with the Nebraska Quilt Project.

Frankie Best.

the bonds forged by the project, whose members still gather regularly."[7]

A quick overview of Frankie Best's quilt reveals the magnitude of arrangements, decisions, energy, and emotion required to undertake a documentation project. Committees were often in place two years before the first quilt was dealt with. These steering committees had to set goals and guidelines, establish procedures, and arrange for help, office space, documentation sites, publicity, and possible sponsorship. They also had to plan for one of the more difficult tasks – funding.

Planning committees, like quilts, were diverse and multi-faceted. Projects were organized by individuals, by quilt guilds, by museums and by programs of oral history. Some committees were directed by boards of as few as three or as many as eighteen. A few projects became membership organizations. In many cases they were separately incorporated which aided in fund-raising once educational status was recognized by the Internal Revenue Service. In most cases a chairperson put together core staffing structures which would help them meet the goals of the intended project. In some instances large state documentation projects appointed regional coordinators who would find local sites and volunteers. The vast distances between state boundaries made for challenges and this alone spoke for the advantages of limited regional studies versus comprehensive statewide ones. A desire for comprehensiveness often won out.

Interest in general quiltmaking was often the criteria for being involved. In some instances experts in such fields as folklore, textiles, quilt conservation and antique quilts, as well as museum personnel and the computer literate, were called on for formulating goals and assisting in training. Groups wrestled with problems and sought advice about liability, insurance, and ethics. Once documentation projects were started, their experience became a resource for other newer projects. "You know how quilters are – they share things and our project was no exception," relates Sandra Todaro of The Louisiana Quilt Search.

Each documentation project had to answer many basic questions concerning the time frame for quilts to be included: would the documentation be limited to quilts brought in during a specific period or would documentation be continuing? Would all quilts in a state be documented or only ones made during a specific period? What kind of information would be collected? Where would this data go during the project and later, when the surveys were complete? Would it be computerized, and if so, by what program and by whom? Who would have access to the information? Would there be a catalog or book? If there was to be a book, who would write it? Who would publish it? What would be included in it? Would there be an exhibit? Where? When? Would it travel? Would any expenses or salaries be paid? Who would pay for them? There were many crucial choices to be made.

The task of funding was monumental. The committees reached out to public institutions and facilities, usually museums, historical societies, or historic sites. Some of these groups were able to provide work space, in-house printing, exhibit facilities, and staff expertise. State quilt guilds and local quilt guilds were able to provide some funding, along with sponsoring quilt days and making quilts for raffle.

The documentation projects sought, and many received, grants from the National Endowment for the Arts, state and local arts organizations, folklife groups, and private foundations. Individuals also made contributions, and sometimes collection boxes were used to solicit public support. The projects sold T-shirts, logo pins, patterns, archival supplies, and photocopies of completed quilt documentation forms and copies of photographs. Auctions of donated small or miniature quilts were sometimes held. In addition those involved often dug deep into their own pockets.

The structure and function of documentation projects varied. The work extended from a brief two years in some cases to more than five in others. But one factor has been the same: volunteerism, which remains the largest single factor in making the documentation projects work.

Nebraska Quilt Project Committee, L to R: Back row: Jo Baxter, Heddy Khol, Doris VonSeggern, Millie Fauquet, Shelly Burge, Janeese Olsson, Pat Caudill Cole, Carroll Dischner, Virginia Welty, MonaJeanne Easter. Middle row: Mary Ghormley, Lois Wilson. Front row: Jean Davie, Frankie Best, Hope Partridge, Sonja Schneider, Pat Hackley, Marlene Marx, Kari Ronning. Not pictured: Jan Stehlik, not available for photo. Mary Obrist, deceased.
Photo: Mark Renkin, Light Impressions Studio, Lincoln, NE.

Chapter 2

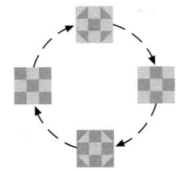

QUILT DOCUMENTATION DAYS
Sharing, Exploring, and Imaging

After goals had been established by the documentation project committee, the primary task then was to find willing local chairpeople. Together with these people they planned a schedule of quilt days, days on which quilt owners were invited to bring their quilts to be documented and photographed. In preparation, corps of workers were trained in documentation, textile dating, and oral interviewing. Most projects identified communities and selected public sites to which quilts would be brought for documentation. Local volunteers were trained close to the time of the event in their region.

At quilt days each quilt brought in was assigned a number and its owner interviewed about its provenance. The quilt was measured and its pattern identified. An expert completed an analysis of its construction techniques and materials, assessed its condition, and established the date it had likely been made. Sometimes an identification label was sewn on. Often the owner was given advice on storage and care. The quilt was then photographed before being sent home with the owner.

After one person at a North Carolina Quilt Documentation Day described the procedure as being "like a mouse going through the snake's belly," the project team put much thought into a more efficient system. Each project learned the best way to keep the process flowing smoothly.

Initially project personnel worried that not enough people would be interested in bringing quilts for documentation, but there are few less-than-successful days on record. Madeline Hawley (Arkansas Quilt Guild, Inc.) tells of their one day when only a few quilts turned up. She literally went up and down the street looking for quilts and happened into a local historical society which had "wonderful" ones. She counted as one of the successes of that day the lesson she gave the curator in proper storage of that cache.

From Quilt Heritage: Washington State, Sally Ambrose tells of their group's readying for a ten o'clock opening. "At 9:30 a.m. *we were inundated* with people and their treasured quilts. All our good procedures, flow charts, and volunteers nearly came unglued." Projects relate experiences of people being lined up before the team even arrived to set up; some found it necessary to impose limits on the number of quilts that could be registered per family.

The scope of the documentation job to be done was not always obvious at first. Sandra Weaver, historian for Region 7 of the Montana Historic Quilt Project, writes of thinking, "How many quilts can be out there. Surely they've all been worn out or loved to death. It won't take long...." Her later thought was: "...my ignorance *is* bliss...in eight months we found out [that] in the cedar chests, trunks, linen closets, beds and front porches where the cat sleeps, there are hundreds of quilts in Big Horn County."

Quilt days were often held in donated space in public places like churches, community centers, historic buildings, clubhouses, and schools. Rooms had to be large enough for groups of tables and also provide space for photography. Most buildings worked just fine. On occasion, however, there was the inevitable snafu. One day in Colorado, quilt owners had to troop through a wedding reception to reach the documentation being held behind a folding partition. Wedding guests drifted in and watched the photography. Members of the Connecticut Project recall the oft unmelodious strains of piano lessons taking place on the other side of a wall, and none who worked with the New York Quilt Project will forget the day that an electrical storm knocked out power to the windowless and multilevel school room they were using. Unable to see, everyone froze in place rather than risk a misstep. According to Phyllis Tepper this was one of two power failures! Mother nature was also responsible for knocking out an air conditioning system on a steamy Georgia day, at which point volunteers "dropped like flies."

Personnel for quilt days were often a combination of the core trained team and members of the group sponsoring that particular day, often a quilt guild, home extension club, or historical society. As Cheryl Kennedy of the Illinois Quilt

Research Project tells it, "The success of each site was clearly dependent on the enthusiasm of our local organizers, and evidence of that enthusiasm can be seen in their numbers." Often local volunteers met with the core team to train an hour or so prior to the arrival of the public. They usually worked at a station with someone who had experience in the procedure. Handouts were sometimes prepared to give volunteers some idea about what to expect. New York went beyond that, preparing a slide show with a script that explained all the stations.

Volunteers needed to have a certain amount of fortitude. Pre-dawn starts with long drives were commonplace. Workers were often on their feet all day long, handling and folding heavy quilts. Allergic sorts learned early on that those who dealt with the quilts often faced clouds of dust, mildew, and spores; blasts of camphor or naphthalene; and even flights of moths. Sometimes cotton backing which had been home dyed brown with walnut hulls suddenly disintegrated in the hands of a shocked volunteer or quilt owner.

Besides stamina, diplomacy and tact were also required in order to deal with those who firmly believed that, because grandmother lived to be 92 and great-grandmother was nearly 100 when she died, a Dresden Plate of soft pastel colors with Nile green sashing, clearly made in the 1930s, "had to be 185 years old." Equal tact was demonstrated in stories of volunteers' dealing with couples who brought quilts from each of their families, and competed to outdo each other in the most significant or beautiful categories. Like snapping terriers they would interrupt, interject, dispute, or correct, and fire epithets about the opposite family branch. Quilt days were meant to display the family quilts, but often they also brought forward the "family linen."

Barbara Lenox, a volunteer with the Lancaster County Quilt Harvest project (PA), recalled one woman she dubbed "the reluctant quilter." That woman did not want to come to a quilt day. Her niece had read about the documentation and was very excited. She literally dragged the aunt along. The older woman very nearly refused to be photographed with her quilt. Barbara reports her relaying that, "when she was a little girl, her quilt block had to be completed before she could go out and play with her brothers....she could point to every block and recount what she missed while she stitched." The woman fairly quivered with indignant emotion as she thought about the ball games, the snowball fights, and the hikes through the woods she had missed. She wanted no reminders of that youthful experience. "You can make a gal stitch fabric, but you can't make her like it," Barbara concluded.

Questions about ethical issues had to be met head on with the commencement of the earliest quilt projects. The biggest worry was one of exposing valuable pieces or collections to public scrutiny. Project boards worried about unscrupulous dealers who might follow quilt owners to make deals just outside the building, taking advantage of those unaware of the current market value of their quilts. The worry was real, but most projects did not actually encounter such situations.

Volunteers willingly signed ethics agreements to keep the information gathered confidential. Many projects banned unofficial photos. Some people did not participate because they were afraid to bring public attention to their holdings, or because they worried other family members might claim ancestral quilts. Happily, few quilt owners were deterred. Most proudly shared their quilts and their family heritage.

Many projects adopted the practice of sewing a permanent label with an identifying number on the back of quilts, so in the future a quilt could be reunited with its written history. The May 1991 issue of the "Washington Quilt Review," the newsletter of Quilt Heritage: Washington State, tells of a crazy quilt top bought in a Washington antique shop by a Maine woman who was able to trace its history because of its identifying label. Interestingly, the woman's daughter married a young man from the very town where the top had been made, so it has now returned "home," history intact. Buyers should be aware, however, that some owners knew nothing about the quilt they had registered, so a project label does not guarantee a complete history.

Quilt days held a magic not unlike that felt by a young child opening gifts. Each unfolded beauty revealed a uniqueness, a surprise, or the predictable sameness that can be so reassuring. A quilt day was a visual phenomena. Each quilt was treated as a treasure: analyzed, then hung for photography; spotlighted for its moments of glory. The public and volunteers alike were often mesmerized by the visual imagery, soon becoming addicted to watching. One Georgia quilt owner sat in the audience and wept openly, overcome by the thought of how proud her grandmother would have felt seeing her quilts honored. Many folks were drawn to the quilts and stayed all day.

Some volunteers were recruited on the spot. They brought quilts to be documented and sensing the need, they pitched in where help was needed that day and sometimes became a part of the team for the next quilt day. One enterprising local coordinator enlisted the services of several young men who were required to perform community service. Anita Weinraub of the Georgia Quilt Project admits, "We always like to grab the young, tall, and spry-looking ones for the photography jobs!" A new arrival from Scotland, Karen Fananapazir, showed up at a quilt day in Durham, North Carolina, thinking it was an exhibit. Not only did she stay and witness the process that particular day, but she also traveled as a loyal team member and even continued to help during the tedious paperwork phase back at the office. Her interest in quilts and new-found knowledge led to contacts and friends in the Washington DC area where she later relocated and still lives. In Georgia, Laura Toney expressed similar sentiments: "We certainly enjoyed our Athens Quilt History Day. My husband and I ended up staying and assisting with the photographing of the quilts. What a joy it was to see the works of art that loving hands had labored to create. An aura surrounded each piece as it was hung."

Plate 2-1.
Utility Quilt.
64" x 79".
c.1920.
Harriet Beckett Austin (1877-1942).
Made in Lick Creek, Summers County, West Virginia.
Top – denim and corduroy. Back – gray chambray. Filling – wool (home processed) tied with twine.
Collection: Juanita Austin Dove Basham.
Photo: Richard Walker.
Documented by the West Virginia Heritage Quilt Search (#6-0199).

Harriet Beckett Austin (1877–1942) of the hilly, rocky farm country of Lick Creek, West Virginia, processed for batting wool shorn from her own sheep. She and her husband, who was also a Baptist preacher and a coffin maker, headed a farm family of six children.

This quilt top is a combination of sturdy denim and corduroy, work clothes material, and is tied with twine. This utility covering with a gray chambray backing was made in about 1920. Such an abstract, exuberant design of limited fabric choices is typical of the many functional quilts of the 1910 through

1950 time period.

Many quilt projects were worried that quilt owners would only bring their fancy quilts to be documented, leaving the heavy, dark ones at home as unworthy of attention. West Virginia was a state that encouraged those with plain quilts to bring them in for documentation. West Virginia project personnel were pleasantly surprised with the wide range and variety of quilts brought in for documentation in their state, and they heard sentiments such as these expressed by this quilt owner: "I feel very fortunate to have this quilt and consider it an honor to be a link in the Austin tradition."

The Austin Family shown in front of their Brown's Ridge, Mercer Co., WV, farmhouse, which was later destroyed by fire. Harriet Beckett Austin (b.1877), the maker of this quilt, is shown seated at right and her husband, Albert Lewis Austin (b.1872), stands to her right in overalls. His father, Albert Galiten Austin (b.1827) stands in front of him in a dark suit. Marie Elizabeth Austin (b.1877), sister of Albert Lewis Austin and mother of the current owner, stands to the far left. This quilt has remained with the family, being passed to the current owner after a cousin's death.

Plate 2-2.
Escher's Triangles #52.
58" x 93".
1989.
Antoinette Mayer.
Made in Washington, DC.
Cottons.
Collection: Steven Mayer.
Photo: Richard Walker.
Documented by the "Made in DC" Quilt Search, Inc.

The "Made in DC" Quilt Search was started by a group of quilt enthusiasts to collect data to help celebrate the founding of Washington as capital of the United States. The group "envisioned quilts of ethnic, regional, and international flavor," according to project head Sue Hannan, who adds: "Instead we found that quilts are, indeed, 'pieces of home' made to give to family members, to enhance our home, to just keep us warm, or to provide a creative outlet."

Washington DC is home to a diverse, international population, and Antoinette Mayer is one of a breed of artistic, disciplined, organized, and creative quiltmakers. Originality of design and color characterize her quilts. She is a self-taught designer and quilter and according to the documentation project is "the most methodical [quilter]...researchers experienced." Each of her quilts is numbered as it is planned. Antoinette takes photos of each quilt in progress and has albums filled with documentation of her more than 90 quilts. "Escher's Triangles" was designed for the entryway of son Steven Mayer's Utah home.

Before hand sewing begins, Antoinette lays out every piece of the quilt on a sheet on the floor of her workroom. She frames each side with a bright yellow pole 1" in diameter. These poles serve as a deterrent to her large gray dog who will not trespass beyond them.

Antoinette Mayer has made Washington DC her home for many years, but she was living in Java at the time of the Japanese invasion during World War II; her father was employed by Shell Oil there, and other relatives were in the Netherlands diplomatic corps. She and her family were made prisoners of war; she in one camp with her sisters, her father in another, and her mother in a third in Borneo. She and her sisters were among a group of women who held on to their sanity in the camp by practicing and performing concerts of classical music, sung unaccompanied and from memory. She and her two sisters survived and were reunited with their mother after the war. The choir's heroic efforts in the camp were documented by a PBS film in 1986. Antoinette finds today's world news events depicting human misery sorrowful and disturbing. Making quilts is her productive distraction.

Fearing overwhelming numbers, most projects limited documentation to quilts made prior to some date within the first half of the twentieth century. The "Made in DC" Quilt Search and a few other documentation projects registered the work of current quiltmakers as well.

Antoinette Mayer, 1982.

Plate 2-3.
Irish Chain.
38" x 73".
1888.
Sarah Pendroy (1826–1902).
Made in Pendroy Post Office, North Dakota (Now Verendrye, North Dakota).
Cottons.
Collection: Marguerite Park.
Photo: Courtesy of the North Dakota Quilt Project.
Documented by the North Dakota Quilt Project (#51-90).

When Sarah Pendroy and her friends sat and quilted her red and white Irish Chain quilt in 1888 they surely had no idea that nearly every North Dakota 8th grader would come to know them from their photograph later included in a widely used classroom history book. The picture was taken in the Pendroy home, which also served as the post office in which her husband James served as postmaster of Pendroy, North Dakota, now Verendrye.

Sarah Jane Baldwin Pendroy had been born in Boardman, Ohio, and died in North Dakota in 1902.

Sarah's granddaughter (the current owner's mother) ensured that her two daughters would both enjoy this legacy by cutting the quilt into two pieces, binding the pieces, and giving one to each daughter. Shown is the half given to Marguerite Park.

Sarah Pendroy and friends quilting at the post office of Pendroy, North Dakota.
Photo: Courtesy of State Historical Society of North Dakota, Bismarck.

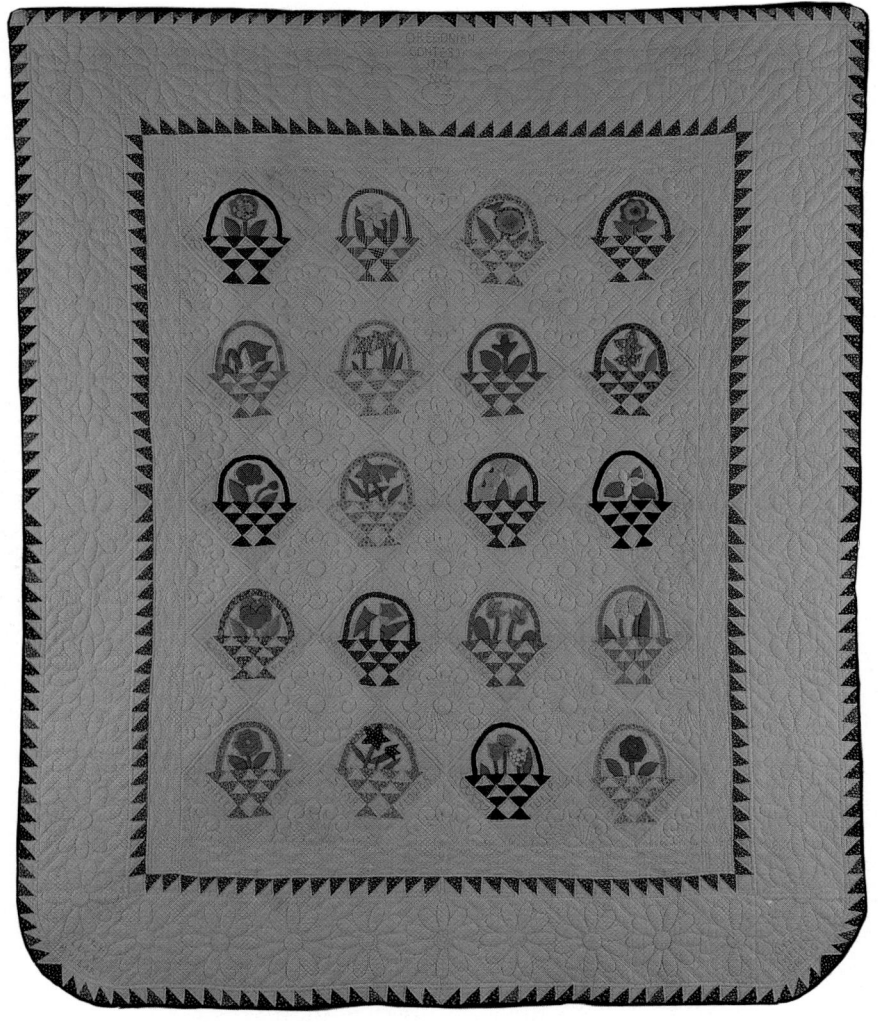

Plate 2-4.
Lucy's Baskets.
86" x 102".
1977.
Pieced by Lucy Puyleart (1889–1972).
Completed by Helen Grigg.
Made in Lake Oswego, Oregon.
Cotton.
Collection: Helen Grigg.
Photo: Richard Walker.
Documented by the Columbia-Willamette Quilt Study Group (Oregonian Newspaper Contest Quilt #3).

Imagine the excitement of receiving a new quilt pattern inside each week's Sunday newspaper. In 1929 the *Oregonian* newspaper ran a series of flower patterns designed to go into pieced basket blocks. To promote newspaper sales locally, a Nancy Page "Grandmother's Garden Contest" was held, with good response. Over 750 entries were displayed at the Portland Gas and Coke Company.

In 1975, to announce the Northwest Quilters Show, a newspaper article appeared seeking examples of the contest quilts and 71 quilt owners responded. In 1985, the Columbia-Willamette Quilt Study Group (CWQSG) held a formal documentation to record each quilt's data. Mary Cross of Portland, a member of the group, presented a paper reporting the findings on thirty of the quilts.

One member of the Columbia-Willamette Quilt Study Group is Helen Grigg of Lake Oswego. In 1977 she assembled and quilted the unfinished work of Lucy Puyleart (1899–1972), creating a quilt she refers to as "Lucy's Baskets" (Plate 2-4). Lucy Puyleart was the daughter of Belgian immigrants who first went to Michigan, then moved on to Irondale, Washington, where she was born, and the following year moved to Lake Oswego, where they farmed. As a child, Lucy and her brothers sold fruits and vegetables door-to-door from a horse-drawn wagon.

Helen Grigg learned to quilt from the Oswego Quilters, a group which started in 1959. "Like any innocent hobby, it took over 43.5% of my life," she recalls. In completing "Lucy's Baskets," Helen chose to stuff the flowers and circles of the Irish Pipe quilting pattern. The Hanging Diamond quilting design is copied from an Egyptian carving found in a tomb.

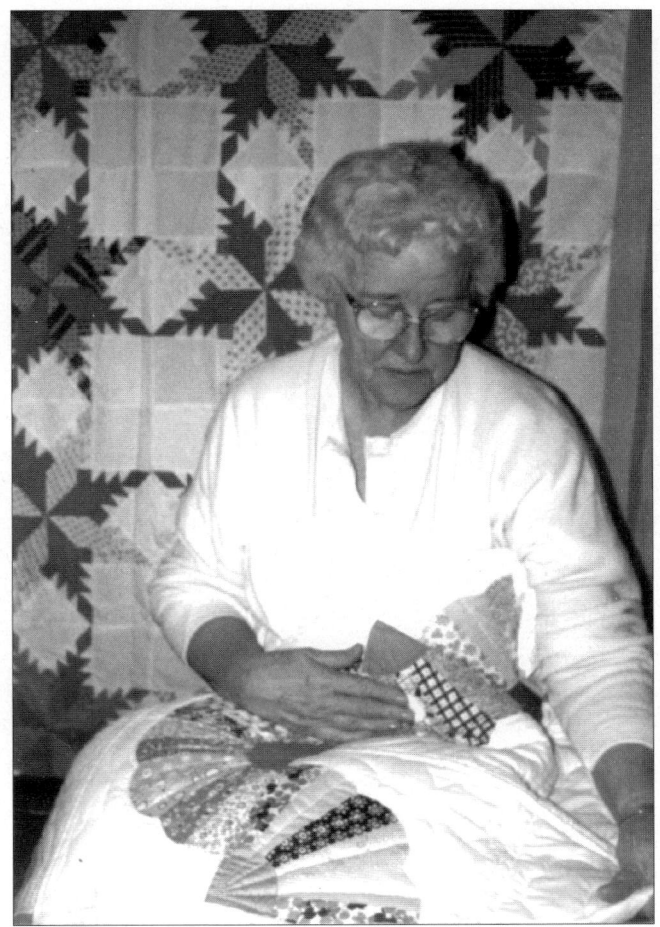

Helen Grigg, Lake Oswego, Oregon, who completed "Lucy's Baskets."

Plate 2-5
Grandmother's Garden
76" x 88".
c.1930.
Hetty Davis Moxley (1890–1983).
Made in Eugene, Oregon.
Cottons.
Collection: Dorothy Zimmerman.
Photo: Richard Walker.
Documented by the Columbia-Willamette Quilt Study Group (Oregonian Newspaper Contest Quilt #1).

Home of Hetty Davis Moxley, as it looked in the 1920's.

Another of the *Oregonian* basket quilts was made by Hetty Davis Moxley (1890–1983) of Goshen, whose grandfather, Dr. Henry A. Davis had come to Oregon from Ohio in 1852. A church quilting group in Eugene did the quilting. The quilt presently belongs to Hetty's niece, Dorothy Zimmerman, another CWQSG member, who spent her summers on the Moxley farm in the southern Willamette Valley and recalls piecing Nine-Patch blocks from her aunt's stash of fabrics.

The daughter of Amelia and Zopher Davis, Hetty was born in Oregon and married Lorenzo Dow Moxley in 1914. The farm couple grew plums. Hetty was an accomplished musician, playing both piano and organ. In her spare time she liked to refinish furniture and make braided rugs. She chose her favorite color combination, orchid and green, for her basket quilt.

Mary Cross put together a comprehensive study of the contest quilts.[1] She explains, "Networking has always been a task I naturally assumed." It was a pleasure for Mary to learn that as a result of her publications, two guilds 2,000 miles apart made raffle quilts from the newspaper patterns. Her interest in documentation continues as she helps develop an Oregon statewide project.

This author happened to be in Salem, Oregon, in 1984 when Mary was giving a lecture on quilting. After a brief introduction as a kindred spirit from North Carolina, the next morning I found myself in Portland, a CWQSG guest. A chance meeting because of a shared interest in quilts has resulted in a lasting relationship – not an uncommon story in the documentation projects.

Drawing from the Sunday OREGONIAN, *May 4, 1975, which appeared with an article to locate original 1929 contest quilts. Quilt shown in the drawing is the pattern used by the contestants.*

Hetty Davis Moxley, maker of "Grandmother's Garden."

Plate 2-7.
Hearts and Gizzards.
72" x 80".
c.1907.
Ida Henderson Shuler (1887–1972).
Made in Walton County, Florida.
Cottons.
Collection: Museum of Florida History.
Photo: Ray Stanyard, courtesy of the Museum of Florida History.
Documented by the Florida Quilt Heritage Project.

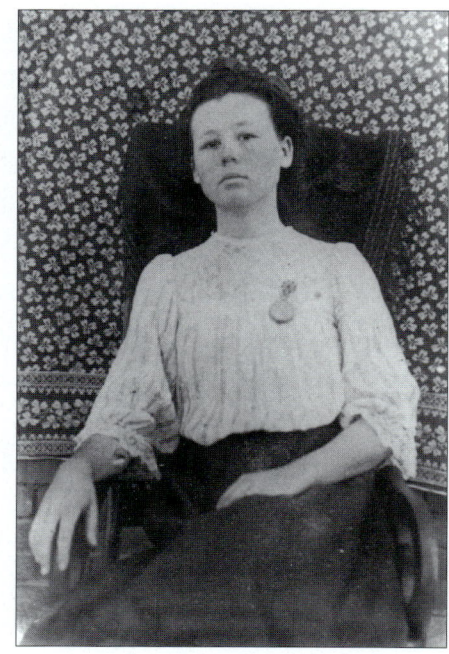

Ida Henderson Shuler. Photo: Courtesy of the Museum of Florida History.

Ida Henderson Shuler (1887–1972) was one of that breed of women who, in order to be content, simply had to stay busy and productive. She was born in Walton County in northwest Florida where as a child she learned quilting from her mother. At 16 she became Gary Shuler's bride. She loved to garden and won many blue ribbons at the county fair for her canned produce. The Shulers grew the cotton for quilt batts and Ida carded it herself.

While proficient in all needlework skills, she loved quilting the best and spent many hours in the front room of her home, often with friends, quilting on a frame suspended from the ceiling. Her quilts were made to be used and were given to family members or to needy persons in the community. At one point in her life when Ida was responsible for running a gristmill, she worked on her quilts between customers. There would be no idleness for Ida!

Most owners whose quilts were included in documentation project exhibits were pleased to have the makers honored and were proud to share their heritage. Exhibit openings were filled with excited anticipation, beaming smiles, reunions, and more than a few tears. Some of the younger viewers realized for the first time their places as links in the ongoing family chain and felt pride and awe in an often heretofore unknown ancestor. As a result of their reactions, sometimes it became obvious within quilt-owning families just which younger member would make the most eager or most capable future caretaker.

Ordinary individuals who just happened to make quilts and never would have sought outside recognition for their domestic feats were honored by all. Many might well have been embarrassed by today's fuss over their doing what was expected during their lifetime.

Jean Shuler Martinec of DeFuniak Springs, Florida, went to see her mother's "Hearts and Gizzards" quilt on display in the "Patches of Sunshine, Patterns of Life," Florida's Quilt Heritage exhibit at the Museum of Florida History in Tallahassee. She was curious as what to expect. Once there, she felt as if she were walking back through a time tunnel. "How could you know she slept on a four poster bed? The kerosene lamp was just like the ones we had in our home so long ago – the half round table was like the one in her home – and what pleased me most of all was the open Bible. How could you know – how could you know?" were some of the words she wrote to the exhibit coordinator after her visit. Jean Martinec seemed to speak for many quilt owners when she added, "All was perfect – and the memory of those few moments I will have for the rest of my life...."

Plate 2-8.
Schoolhouse Scrap Quilt.
81" x 67".
1900.
Hannah Stone.
Made in Belle Plaine, Iowa.
Cotton.
Collection: Harold and Dorothy Birky
Photo: Richard Walker.
Documented by the Iowa Quilt Research Project (#H-13).

Harold and Dorothy Birky, the current owners. Harold is a descendant of Hazel Fisher Birky, one of the sisters pictured.

As individual projects collected data, trends in style, pattern choice, and color preferences began to emerge. The tremendous growth of public education during the third quarter of the nineteenth century resulted in the pieced Schoolhouse block pattern becoming popular with quiltmakers. An unusual medallion rendition was made during that time period in Belle Plaine, Iowa, by Hannah Stone. Born in the 1860s and known as "Aunty Stone," oral tradition says that the quilt was specially created for the wedding of Hannah's son, Richard Bostain, to Mabel Fisher. The Benton County farm couple lived a simple lifestyle without the benefit of electricity, even though the line ran along the road near their farm. Plowing was done with horses and they ventured into town only occasionally for groceries.

The quilt was acquired by its present owners at auction. Dorothy Birky would like to think that 90 years hence the quilts she's making "… will be in as good condition as our little prized quilt."

Many quilt documentation projects adopted the pattern identification system developed in Barbara Brackman's *Encyclopedia of Pieced Quilt Patterns* as a standard for assigning names. Few other pattern sources were so comprehensive, allowing for the interpolation of standard pattern types to identity related variations. Owners were anxious to learn names for patterns so they could feel more knowledgeable about their family quilts, in spite of the fact that many of these quilts had never been referred to by their makers by a pattern name. The assignment of quilt names to be used as titles, though not necessarily historically valid, was also necessary to create a data field for computerization purposes.

Mabel Fisher is shown with her sisters and mother. Front: Mabel, Florence, Mother, Hazel, and Bessie Fisher; Back: Ethel, Mamie, and Ruth Fisher. This Schoolhouse Scrap Quilt is said to have been made for Mabel Fisher, upon her marriage to the maker's son, Richard Bostain.

Plate 2-9.
Geometry Sampler.
71" x 104".
1935.
Pawnee, Oklahoma High School
    Geometry Class of 1935.
Quilted by Mrs. L. P. (Helen) Saunders.
Made in Pawnee, Oklahoma.
Cotton.
Collection: Clella Harris Kelley.
Photo: Richard Walker.
Documented by the Oklahoma Quilt Heritage
    Project.

Kathryn Cunningham had an innovative method of helping her students understand geometry. Photo: courtesy of the Pawnee County Historical Society.

It was a creative experience to be in Kathryn Cunningham's 1935 geometry class at Pawnee High School Pawnee, Oklahoma. That year the students pieced a quilt by making blocks which taught some of the principles of geometry.

When Madge Amspacher of the Oklahoma City area spied the picture of the "Geometry Sampler Quilt" in a friend's copy of *Oklahoma Heritage Quilts*, vivid memories of the quilt block assignment came rushing forth. She had been 14 at the time. Each student designed and then sewed a block and embroidered his or her initials on it. She related that the students' initials were done like a monogram, with the last initial in the middle, a conventional style at the time.

The top was quilted by Helen Saunders and stayed in the teacher's possession until given to Clella Harris Kelley, the current owner. The quilt is now at the Pawnee County Historical Society, Pawnee, OK, where the makers and their families can see it.

Volunteers during the documentation project commented that if they had been taught quilting along with geometry they might have developed totally different attitudes toward math. Clella Harris Kelley comments that "for some unknown reason Miss Cunningham never repeated the project."

In 1983 students of the "Geometry Sampler Quilt" class posed with the handmade quilt which was designed in Miss Kathryn Cunningham's PHS geometry class. Members of the class present for this photo include Franklin (Hank) Hartwick, standing left, Maxine (Hines) Rice, seated left, Clella (Harris) Kelley, seated right, and Ruby (Beaver) Johnston, standing right. Photo: courtesy of the Pawnee County Historical Society.

Plate 2-10.
Hawaiian Flag Quilt.
78" x 80".
c.1900.
Maker unknown.
Probably made in Honolulu, Oahu.
Cotton fabric, wool batting.
Collection: Mr. and Mrs. Allen Wall.
Photo: Richard Walker.
Documented by the Hawaiian Quilt Research Project (#514).

Perhaps no other Hawaiian quilt type has evoked as much emotion, speculation, and secrecy as the Hawaiian Flag Quilt. Many examples contain the lettering *KU'U HAE ALOHA* meaning *My Beloved Flag*. While the exact story of this particular flag quilt has been lost as it has been passed down through the family, there are certain consistent characteristics of Hawaiian flag quilts. Hawaiian quilts have traditionally used symbols which express the monarchy, such as the center crown surrounded by a butterfly, which depicts a favorite butterfly hair adornment of Queen Lili'uokalani, Hawaii's last reigning monarch.

Flag quilts were made in Hawaii prior to 1850, but there was a resurgence of flag quilts, similar to this one, during the period when Queen Lili'uokalani was deposed (1893) and the islands were annexed by the United States in (1898). As reminders of the lost kingdoms, they contain symbols of the Hawaiian monarchy such as coats of arms, crowns, fans, and wreaths. Abiding examples of Hawaiian culture and history, flag quilts have become a vehicle for those quiltmakers and subsequent generations wanting to represent their cultural identity, pride, and resourcefulness.

The Hawaiian Quilt Research Project is unique in that it restricts documentation to Hawaiian Style appliqué quilts and Hawaiian flag quilts made prior to 1960.

Plate 2-11.
Say Cheese.
81" x 91".
1994.
Made by Volunteers of the Georgia Quilt Project.
Made in Georgia.
Cottons.
Collection: William C. L. (Bill) Weinraub.
Photo: Charley Lynch.
Made in conjunction with the Georgia Quilt Project.

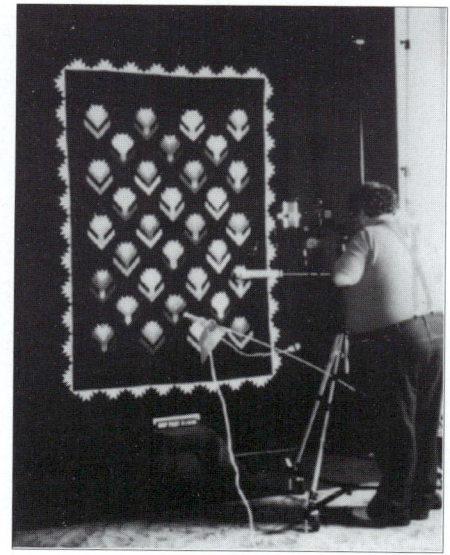

William C. L. (Bill) Weinraub at work during a quilt day. Photo courtesy of the Georgia Quilt Project.

Real estate investor William C.L. (Bill) Weinraub has had to play a dual role with the Georgia Quilt Project. The first is as husband to Anita, the project chairperson. Rather than waiting at home, Bill became the project photographer. This second role rekindled an old interest and provided him with the perfect excuse to upgrade his camera equipment. He was literally the only volunteer who had to be at each quilt day. He had to be there early to set up and stay late to see that all quilts had been photographed. During the three-year documentation period, Bill was there for 73 of the 76 documentation days held.

The usual quilt day procedure in Georgia was to have the day's sponsoring organization provide lunch for the volunteers. Those repasts became Bill's introduction to pimiento cheese sandwiches. For a New-York-state-bred boy, this was a new culinary experience. The only pimiento cheese he had seen had come in a squirt can. Bill began to develop a fondness for this spread made with prized, made-from-scratch recipes.

Volunteers were inspired to make Bill a quilt in appreciation for his hard work – one with pimiento cheese as its theme. Letters invited photography volunteers from all over Georgia to make eight-inch blocks. Those who didn't make blocks signed their names and towns on muslin strips. Pam Winberg and other Gwinnett Quilt Guild members put the blocks together into five mini tops which were then incorporated in the top. Other blocks were placed on the back. The quilt made the rounds of many guilds to be basted and quilted.

At a project reunion held under the ruse of promised good food, good company, and no work, Bill was presented his quilt on August 18, 1994. In the center was his wife Anita's block, a cheddar-colored rendition of a pattern known as Contrary Wife.

Bill was totally surprised and deeply touched. He writes: "I rarely think of myself as selfless or particularly dedicated. As I see it, my tenure as GQP's marathon quilt photographer is really characterized as one of irascible, cantankerous, obstreperous, recalcitrant, overbearing drill-sergeantry in which I browbeat good-natured, overworked, under thanked, occasionally dilatory but predominantly compliant, devoted volunteer ladies (and the odd captive husband) mercilessly for hours and even days at a time." Bill will always relish his "Say Cheese" quilt – the Bed Spread.

Projects lasted for as few as 2½ years to as many as eight. From 1980 until 1994 more than 12,775 volunteers had taken part in the effort. Throughout the information gathering phase of the projects plans were formulated for exhibitions of selected quilts and for the publication of a book. These varied from brief catalogs to serious evaluations of survey findings. Georgia's book, with its photos by Bill Weinraub, will be published in 1996.

Plate 2-12.
Tulip Quilt.
82" x 89".
1847.
Elizabeth Jane Wymer Crabill (1825–1904).
Made in Tom's Brook, Virginia.
Cottons, muslin.
Collection: Roger Crabill.
Photo: Richard Walker.
Documented by the Virginia Quilt Research Project (#A-177).

What quilt in "GATHERINGS: America's Quilt Heritage" could better represent the Virginia Quilt Research Project than one inscribed "MADE IN VA" in a center block. Along with this inscription are the initials EJC and the date 1847, all rendered in a satin stitch. The maker of this red and green Tulip or Lily quilt was Elizabeth Jane Wymer Crabill. Born in 1825 in Shenandoah County to John and Rebecca Wymer, she and her husband George Keller Crabill lived near Tom's Brook. George was a farmer and carpenter and they had six children. Both her husband and their son Benjamin served in the Confederate forces, George in Co. B. 33 Inf, Benjamin in the "Laurel Brigade," Co. E, 11th Virginia Cavalry.

Chapter 3

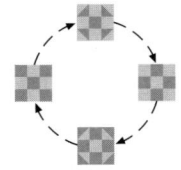

QUILTS AND THEIR MAKERS
Infinite Varieties

Quilts made in the past would often have remained anonymous, ultimately lost from knowledge, were it not for the state documentation projects. Many of the quilts which follow were made in the nineteenth and early years of the twentieth century. It is precisely these quilts which projects set out to find, register, and document. None-the-less, the stories of quilts and quiltmakers which had the richest detail were often, not surprisingly, those made after World War I.

Sometimes when quilts were documented, everything that could possibly be known about that quilt and its maker was offered by the owner. Many brought along printed family geneologies and photo albums and were explicit about when the quilt was made, often linking it to a specific occasion. Other times, the owners could offer limited information or none at all. It was then up to the documenter to venture a reasonable date for when a quilt could have been made based on its style, materials, and pattern.

Phyllis Thompson encountered an interesting phenomenon in the Lancaster County Quilt Harvest (PA) which may account for some quilts with unknown makers. She discovered the custom there is for possessions to "go to sale" or auction after the death of an owner. If a family wants any item they must purchase it at the auction. Phyllis comments, "No wonder we have so many quilts floating around Lancaster County where the maker's identity is lost." The tradition of such auctions was one of the topics presented at the Oral Traditions Symposium held at Franklin and Marshall College in Lancaster in 1993.[1]

The heightened awareness of quilts as important objects of material culture has created additional responsibility for collectors and institutions alike to record when possible the social history and provenance of each new acquisition. For this reason, nowadays institutions are frequently hesitant to accept donations of quilts for which such information is not available.

Plate 3-1.
Four Flower Pots Appliqué.
68" x 81".
1854.
Elizabeth Ann Shipman Powell.
Made in Dugger, Indiana.
Cotton.
Collection: Indiana State Museum (#71.979.23.5).
Photo: Indiana State Museum.
Documented by the Indiana Quilt Registry Project.

A quilt known to the family as "Fancy Know Nothing" was one of seven quilts – and the only appliquéd one – in the group given to the Indiana State Museum. It was made in 1854 by Elizabeth Ann Shipman Powell of Dugger, Indiana. The four large pots are surrounded by an elegant scalloped swag border.

Plate 3-2.
Reverse Appliqué.
69" x 76".
c.1860.
Narcissa L. Erwin Black(1810–1894) and/or Chany Scott Black (1818–).
Made in McNairy County, Tennessee.
Cotton.
Collection: Mississippi State Historical Museum (#87.42.1)
Photo: Mississippi Department of Archives and History.
Documented and submitted by the Mississippi State Historical Museum.

Three diverse quilts — a Log Cabin, a machine appliquéd floral design, and an unusual red and white reverse appliqué — are part of a family collection in the Mississippi State Historical Museum. The quilts were made by Narcissa L. Erwin Black (1810–1894) and/or Chany Scott Black (1818–?). Narcissa was a skilled seamstress. Chany was an expert weaver. Though originally mistress and slave, these McNairy County (TN) women had a relationship which included extensive business dealings and a close personal friendship. Because Narcissa Black kept a diary which additionally included all of her textile related business accounts, much is known about her life from 1861–1886.

The daughter of Nathaniel and Mary Erwin, Narcissa was born in Sumner County, Tennessee, in 1810 and later moved west with her family to McNairy County. There she married John H. Black in 1836. Black was the son of a plantation owner and 1860 records indicate that he owned four slaves, including Chany and her sons Porter and Albert. Chany and Narcissa worked together on tasks from sheep shearing and thread spinning to dyeing, weaving, and sewing. Narcissa traded in both goods and labor. When John Black died in 1865, the income from Narcissa's textile activity was critical to her livelihood. As head of a household, Chany, too, struggled to achieve a living. Narcissa's diary tells of Chany's purchasing her own loom and having a house raising. The two women continued as partners until 1872 when Chany moved away, probably as a result of Klan activity targeted at her son.

Although Narcissa's diary makes no specific reference to an individual quilt, there are many entries about she and Chany working together on quilts as well as attending and hosting quiltings. This reverse appliqué quilt, with its cutout hearts, horseshoes, and stars, is a remarkable tribute to its two talented makers. After 1872 no word was heard again of Chany. Narcissa remarried in 1878 and died at 83 in 1894, having outlived a second husband. Her diary is an important chronicle of the lives of two talented and industrious women.[1a]

1 January 1861 – This is a beautiful day, we are all well, and all at home, Robert and Lizzie were married the 25th day of December, and are living here, Sara Carman is here framing my Quilt, Chaney is spooling her dresses.

Narcissa L. Erwin Black.

The first entry in her diary. Collection of the Mississippi Department of Archives and History.

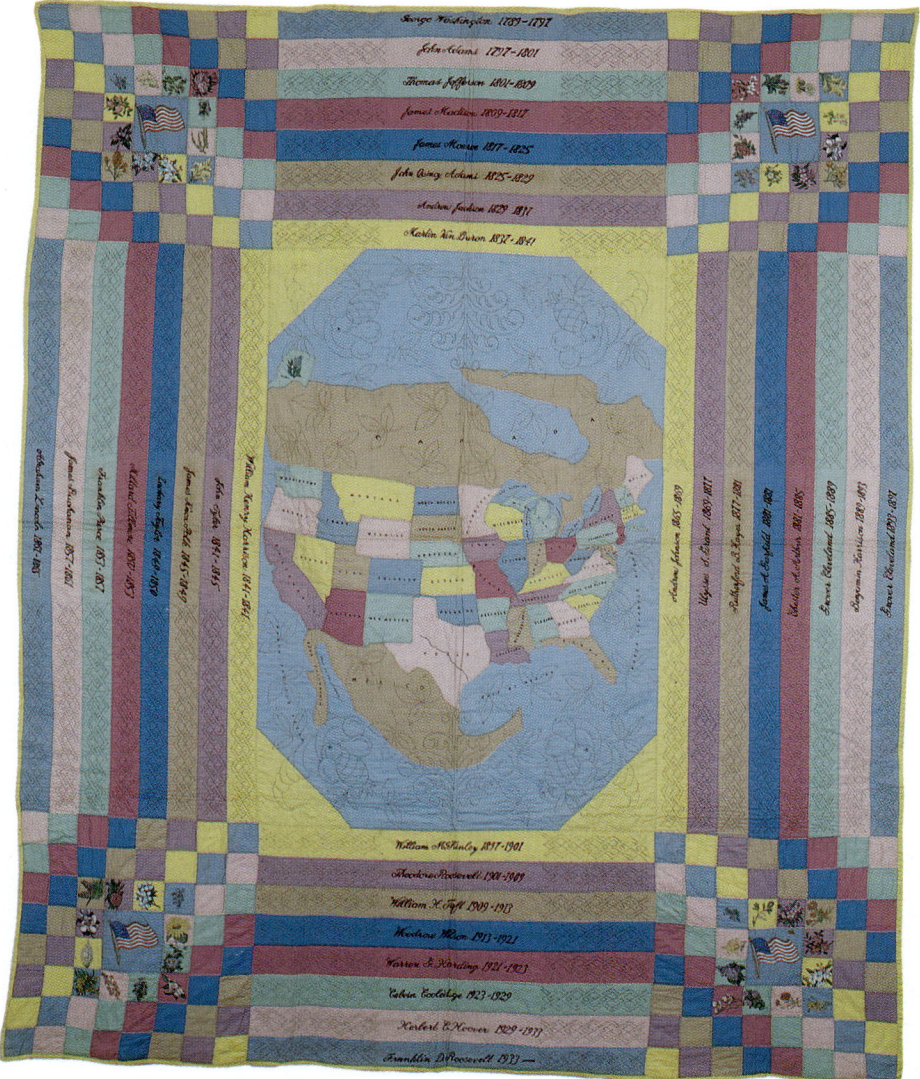

Plate 3-3.
Map of U.S.A.
77" x 92".
1933.
Mrs. Charles (Estella Gwyn) Frick (1878–1951).
Made in New Orleans and Mandeville, Louisiana.
Cotton.
Collection: Patricia Reno.
Photo: Charley Lynch.
Documented by the Louisiana Quilt Search (#1252).

The Sears Roebuck and Company Chicago World's Fair Contest of 1933 drew over 24,000 entries from all over the nation. The company estimates that they had an entry from one in every 2,000 American women — an unheard of response that has never been equaled in American quilt history.

For a nation in the throes of the Great Depression, prizes totaling $7,500 were incentive enough for many to drop everything and make a quilt. The contest was announced in January 1933 and entrants had only until May 15 to enter their quilts.

The theme of the contest was A Century of Progress, following the emphasis of the Chicago World's Fair, which was celebrating that city's one hundredth birthday. Winners of the quilt contest were exhibited at the Sears Pavilion. Quilts were entered at the local Sears retail store or mail order house, with three winners being selected at each store and ten at the mail order facility. Local prizes were $5 or $10 each. From there, winners went on to one of ten regional competitions from each of which three champions proceeded to the national competition. Response was such that the Atlanta store alone received 1,100 entries. It was a contest that "would certainly promote sales of fabric and quilt patterns."[2]

One contestant was Ella Estella (Stella) Gywn Frick (1878–1951) of Louisiana. She designed a quilt depicting a map of the United States. A pieced border surrounded the appliqué center and was embroidered with the names of the presidents. While it was not a Sears winner, this quilt is still accompanied by a Blue ribbon 1st premium won at the Fair in Donaldsonville in 1933.

Illinois-born Stella was one of ten children of Rebecca Greer and Wilson Grey Gwyn. She met her future husband, Charles Henry Frick, in Litchfield, Illinois, in 1896 when they both played drums in a parade honoring President William McKinley. The couple relocated to Louisiana in 1900 where Dr. Frick, a dentist, opened an office in New Orleans. At the time of their move, their only child Alma was a six-week-old infant who made the journey carried on a pillow. Over the years Stella made many quilts and enjoyed hand work.

Criticism about the winning quilts in the Sears contest was voiced in many circles since innovative patterns depicting the Century of Progress theme, as opposed to traditional ones, were virtually ignored. One disgruntled contestant from Chicago wrote that she found the grand prize winner "ordinary" she added, "I thought they were looking for something that was unique."[3]

Dr. Charles H. Frick, daughter Alma and Estella Gwyn Frick. c.1904.

Plate 3-4.
Silk and Velvet Crazy Quilt.
72" x 87".
c.1897.
Richardson sisters:
    Victoria R. Johnson (1863-1942),
    Laura Violet Richardson (1874-1955),
    Mary Valeria Richardson (1881-1966).
Made in Cheyenne, Wyoming.
Silk, Cotton, and wool.
Collection: Wyoming State Museum.
Photo: Wyoming State Museum.
Submitted by the Wyoming State Museum for
    their collection. (#67.130.89)

It is perhaps difficult to imagine a staid, Victorian lifestyle in the wild west of Wyoming, a place of cattle and sheep ranching, but such a quiet, cultured, and circumspect mode existed for the Richardson sisters of Cheyenne. In 1869 their father, Warren Richardson, was sent by *The Rocky Mountain News* to the Wyoming Territory, to establish a newspaper. This was the year that marked the completion of the first rail line in Wyoming and the election of the state's first territorial legislature. His wife and three young children, including a daughter Victoria, soon followed from Indiana. Laura, Valeria, and two other brothers were born later in Cheyenne. The family unit was close and rather closed.

The Richardson brothers were encouraged to be outgoing and adventurous entrepreneurs, and with their father they soon amassed a multi-million dollar fortune. The sisters' lives were channeled inward, ironic in light of Wyoming's being the first state to grant full women's suffrage. Their only socializing was to host small teas and luncheons, and they were described as "old world stay-at-homes," although gracious hostesses. Victoria did marry in 1886 but continued to maintain close ties with her family. Each sister had favorite civic organizations. Victoria's included the Cheyenne Pioneer Women's Club. Laura was a member of St. Mark's Episcopal Guild and the DAR, and was a patron of the Center for the Blind.

Together, the Richardson children established a clinical laboratory at Memorial Hospital in memory of their mother, and endowed a scholarship for a Cheyenne student to attend the University of Wyoming. Laura, Valeria, and brothers Warren, Jr. and Clarence lived together in the family home in relative seclusion until their deaths. Valeria, the last surviving sibling died in 1966.

The Richardson sisters' crazy quilt was made in about 1897. It is unusual in that it appears to have been constructed as an entire unit rather than in squares. It contains personalized embroidery and commemorative ribbons. One ribbon recognizes the performance of Lucia di Lammermore with Mlle. Emma Nevada at the Cheyenne Opera House, an event the Richardsons undoubtedly attended.

Valeria, Victoria, and Laura Richardson.
Photo: Courtesy of Wyoming State Museum.

Plate 3-5.
Album.
70" x 90".
c.1850.
Betsy Jane Young Luce (1833–1887).
Made in Riverhead, New York.
Cotton.
Collection: Beth Dettner.
Photo: Richard Walker.
Documented by the New York Quilt Project (#LIP42NY).

A quilt which reflects the social, economic, and geographic flavor of a community is represented by an eastern Long Island, New York, Album Quilt made by Betsy Jane Young Luce (1833–1887). Near the quilt's center is the grange hall which was moved from the town of Riverhead to the hamlet of Sound Avenue. Once relocated, a steeple was added to the structure and it became First Parish Congregational Church. The church served as the center of the family's social life. The mother of twelve, including two sets of twins, Betsy Jane was the wife of Hallock Luce. The family grew potatoes in this area known for produce farms.

The "Album Quilt" also reflects the maritime atmosphere of the area and includes appliqués of a fish, a mariner's compass, and a sextant star. It also incorporates an oak leaf typical of the kind indigenous to Long Island, and various local flowers. The quilt has remained within the area in which it was made and has passed on to female family members with the given name of Betsy and Beth.

Today, the grange hall which became a church still stands and serves as the Sound Avenue neighborhood meeting hall. The present quilt owner, Beth Dettner, Betsy Jane Luce's great-granddaughter, has carried on the family tradition of quiltmaking and is a member of the Eastern Long Island Quilt Guild. She was also a volunteer in a number of documentation days. The "Album Quilt" is slated to go to her daughter, Mary Beth Mack and then to her granddaughter Nora Beth Mack.

Betsy Jane Young Luce (1833–1887).

Plate 3-6.
Double X.
64" x 76".
c.1897.
Julia Ann Mills Trueblood.
Made in Iowa.
Cottons.
Collection: Leota M. Hopp / Irma L. Davis.
Photo: Richard Walker.
Documented by the Texas Quilt Search.

Julia Ann Mills Trueblood.

"We had a happy family life" reported Leota Trueblood Hopp when she was interviewed in 1986 by Sharon L. Newman of the Prairie Windmill Quilt History and Research Chapter, NQA. Leota recalled that her mother, Julia Ann Mills Trueblood had lots of "pep and energy," was "kind and gentle," and was "never idle." Born February 11, 1872, to David and Margaret Hockett Mills near Salem, Iowa, at age 19 Julia married W. Foster Trueblood. The couple farmed in both Iowa and Missouri until their retirement. Julia had beautiful flower gardens and used her boundless energy sewing and caring for her children. She often read to them and made each a full-sized quilt using scraps from their baby clothes. But life for Julia Trueblood was not without its heartbreak and trials. Her first two boys died as infants. Later, nine-year-old Ernie drowned, and Arlo, as a young adult, was killed in a farming accident.

Arlo's quilt "Double X" had been made about 1898 or 1899, much of it from 20-year-old scraps given to Julia by her mother after an 1896 fire had destroyed Julia's own fabric supply. Julia was very partial to patterns containing triangles. She took great care in her fabric selection and choice of quilting design. The children each received a large-sized bed quilt rather than a crib quilt.

Julia was able to purchase most of her quilting fabric, batting, and supplies in the local store in Oakland Mill, a small town near the Skunk River in Iowa. She was adept at making her own quilting patterns and adjusting them to the needed size. She taught both Leota and her sister Elsie to make quilts and on extended visits to their homes would often work with each of them on quilts. As a bride in 1932 Leota moved to Texas and brought with her a number of quilts. Others were added later because Julia could never be satisfied without quilting to do. She and Elsie had an ongoing competition to see who could make a quilt with the most pieces. Julia produced full-sized Double Wedding Ring quilts in miniature scale for her eldest grandchildren. Skill and a sense of beauty were combined qualities in Julia Trueblood's life. She always looked on the bright side and upon her death in 1958 left a legacy of superlative quiltmaking.

Plate 3-7.
Triple Star.
93" x 73" (shown sideways).
c.1880.
Elizabeth Cope Graves (1827–1914).
Made in Fairdealing, Missouri.
Cotton.
Collection: Edith M. Leeper.
Photo: Courtesy of The American Quilter's Society.
Documented by the Missouri Heritage Quilt Project.

Elizabeth Cope Graves (1827–1914) married her husband Peter in North Carolina and moved to Tennessee in a covered prairie schooner drawn by oxen. They brought the home fire with them, in an iron kettle which swung by a pole. They lived for a while in Tennessee before continuing on to Fairdealing, Missouri, in 1854. The home fire was carried on that leg of the journey as well.

The couple applied for and received a land grant. The papers were signed by James Buchanan. In every respect, they were a true pioneer couple. They grew all their own food and crafted all their own tools and implements. Elizabeth had learned her skills and knowledge of color and patterns in North Carolina. Resourceful, she grew her own cotton and flax, and raised her own sheep. She spun, wove, and dyed her own cloth, but preferred store-bought prints for her quilts. The quilt batting was prepared at home from her own harvest.

A prolific quiltmaker, she helped her three daughters prepare quilts, coverlets, and blankets for their hope chests. Each daughter had enough bed covers for her future practical needs as well as quilts Elizabeth had worked on as an expression of her personal achievement. Her "Triple Star" reveals both skill and creativity.

Elizabeth Cope Graves (1827–1914).

Plate 3-8.
Silk Mosaic.
(detail, pieced center)
103" x 97".
1852.
Marina Jones Gregg.
Made in Charleston County, South Carolina.
Silk, taffeta, and silk brocade.
Collection: The Charleston Museum.
Photo: Terry Richardson, Charleston, SC, courtesy of The Charleston Museum.
Documented by the South Carolina Quilt History Project.

Detail showing quilted border and fringe that complete the quilt.

A 1928 biography of textile industrialist William Gregg refers to this South Carolina mill owner as the "South's first great bourgeois, the forerunner of a new era."[4] He was well traveled and made his home on Calhoun Street in Charleston for sixteen years. There, continues the biographer, "He had a beautiful home, and interesting friends aplenty."[5] With the family living in such affluent and privileged circumstances, it is understandable that an elegant and sophisticated hexagon quilt of rich silks could be made by his wife, Marina Jones Gregg (c.1812 –)

Marina was the eldest daughter of Colonel Matthias Jones, who kept a store at Ridge Spring in the Edgefield District of South Carolina. She married William Gregg in 1829 when she was seventeen. They lived in Columbia, where William was a silversmith and jeweler who amassed considerable wealth. In 1838 the family, including by then three children, moved to Charleston. With his brother-in-law Tillman Watson, William Gregg founded in Aiken the Graniteville Manufacturing Company, the state's first successful cotton mill.

This silk hexagon quilt was completed in 1852 and represents a type found specifically in the sophisticated port city of Charleston. According to quilt researcher Laurel Horton, examples of quilts made using templates or the English paper piecing method of construction are infrequent in other parts of the state, but they actually survived the Civil War period here, continuing until the 1880s when crazy quilts became popular in Charleston.[6] Marina Gregg chose thread to match the colors of each piece. The border was quilted in a flowing cable design, and the edges of the quilt were finished with long fringe. For her masterpiece, Marina Gregg received a Best Quilt award from the Southern Central Agricultural Society in 1852.

The Gregg family soon moved back upstate so William Gregg could be closer to his business ventures. He later became a member of the South Carolina Secession Convention. The collapse of the South's economy ruined his businesses and dealt devastating personal financial blows. William Gregg died in 1867, and in declining health, Marina Gregg returned to Charleston in 1870. Gregg's biographer describes her at the time as "her same calm self, accepting her deprivations with composure. [She] took to her room for the rest of her life." He also goes on to describe a photograph taken before the move depicting her as "the little old lady in lace cap and mittens, knitting. She was a celebrated knitter of baby socks, and made them for her great-grandchildren."[7] Small-scale, precise work appears to have been her forte.

Plate 3-9.
Dove in the Window.
69" x 80".
c.1834.
Sarah Middleton Lloyd (1808–?).
Made in Pennsylvania.
Wool (hand made by quiltmaker).
Collection: Charlene Javernick &
　Evelyn Whittington.
Photo: Richard Walker.
Documented by the Boise Basin Quilters Guild
　Registration Project (#01896).

Laura Lloyd Barron moved west to Idaho about 1910. She brought with her a family heirloom – a quilt made by her grandmother.

Sarah Middleton Lloyd and her husband Watts B. Lloyd were a Pennsylvania farm couple from the Waterford Township of Erie County. Sarah was born in 1808 in Pennsylvania; Watts had been born a year earlier in neighboring New York State. Together they raised a dozen children.

A note attached to the quilt reads as follows: "Made by Sarah Middleton Lloyd for her 'hope chest' about the Year 1834. The wool was carded, spun, and dyed by her, the cloth woven, and pieced and quilted. Also filled with carded wool from the home flock. The pattern is 'Dove in the Window.' Property of Laura Lloyd Barron."

This classic pattern is also known as Wandering Foot or Turkey Track. The strong Zigzag border, the subtle home-dyed colors, and home-loomed cloth make this quilt exceptional. Enhancing its physical attributes are the pride and interest shown by the present owners, the quiltmaker's great-great-granddaughters.

Sarah Middleton Lloyd.

Plate 3-10.
Illinois Sampler Quilt.
81" x 96".
1977-1988.
Laurel Bangert Goff (1953-).
Made in Springfield, Illinois.
Cottons.
Collection: Laurel Bangert Goff.
Photo: Richard Walker.
Documented by the Illinois Quilt Research Project.

Laurel Bangert Goff.

Laurel Goff's sampler quilt was made from blocks produced over an eleven-year period. These blocks were experiments, mistakes, and extras. She also made an extra block for each of her new quilts to help her remember them. The Pine Tree Medallion was part of a never-finished baby quilt; the hearts are from an appliqué lesson. The cat is Mr. Barnes, who was lying on the quilt one day in typical feline fashion; it seemed logical to copy him.

A self-taught quiltmaker, Laurel dedicated this quilt to her maternal grandmother, Josephine Hufford Ashcraft, with whom she spent much time. Laurel watched her grandmother sew, but explains, "she never intentionally taught me. She was a distant woman. Her laughter was buried under a life of hard work." Laurel wishes her grandmother, who died when Laurel was only 9, could smile about this recognition. Laurel believes she inherited strength and nimble fingers from this ancestor. Years of watching this grandmother sew certainly left an indelible impression.

Laurel quilts on a frame made especially for her by her brother, Thomas Ashcraft, who encourages and confirms her interest. Of all her works, "Illinois Sampler Quilt" holds the most meaning for her, and she hopes that her four children will vie for it someday.

Presently working on her twentieth bed-size quilt, Laurel is president of her Springfield (IL) quilt guild. She admits that "people who started quilting later missed out on the pure haphazard experimenting that had to be part of the process in the 1960s and most of the 1970s. Pattern templates were cut from cereal boxes, and not much in the line of 100 percent cottons was available. Books were scarce, too. Now it's heaven with all the choices in quilter's tools and supplies. But the guess work and improvisation (that were necessary then) were fun and made inventors out of every quilter."

c.1935. Josephine Pearl Hufford Ashcraft (1885–1963), the grandmother to whose memory Laurel Bangert Goff dedicated this quilt.

Plate 3-11.
Postage Stamp Quilt.
83" x 82".
Pieced 1890-1893; completed recently.
Frank Taber (1859-1893).
Made in Medfield, Massachusetts.
Cotton.
Collection: Mrs Howard N. (Dorothy J.) Kane.
Photo: Charley Lynch.
Submitted by the Medfield, Massachusetts Quilt Documentation, to be incorporated in MASS Quilts: The Massachusetts Quilt Documentation Project.

Frank Howard Taber (1859–1893).

Frank Howard Taber and his brother Will were brought up by their young mother, a Civil War widow. Their father had been captured at the Battle of Brandy Station and later died at Andersonville Prison. Both boys were musical. Will was a well-known organist and choir director. Frank gave concerts on the zither at local entertainment evenings.

Until disabled by consumption in 1890, Frank had been employed as a bookkeeper at the Medfield Straw Hat Factory (MA). In order to help the time pass, as an invalid Frank began piecing quilts on a treadle machine. In all, his "Postage Stamp Quilt" has 7,569 pieces. Frank, his wife Clara, and their two young daughters lived close to the railroad tracks. As word got out about Frank and his quilts, engineers on the railroad would signal Clara and then drop bundles of their wives' sewing scraps as the train moved slowly through town.

Frank Taber died in 1893 in his 34th year, leaving unfinished a smaller quilt top with a commemorative print from the World's Columbian Exposition (Chicago) of 1893 in the center (above right). The backing and border on the "Postage Stamp Quilt" were added recently to help preserve the top.

An unfinished postage stamp piece by Frank Taber which includes in its center a souvenir print from the World's Columbian Exposition (Chicago) of 1893.
Photo: Charley Lynch.

Dorothy J. Kane, owner and granddaughter of the maker.
Photo: Ray Warburton.

Clara, wife; Abbie, mother; Ethel, daughter; and Frank H. Taber, shown in front of Frank's "Postage Stamp Quilt" (color photo of quilt shown on page 68).

Plate 3-12.
Whig's Defeat.
93" x 94"
c.1880.
Emma Hardin Burris (1855–1902).
*Made in Turkey Creek, York County,
    South Carolina.*
Cotton.
Collection: York County Historical Commission.
Photo: Charley Lynch.
*Documented by the South Carolina Quilt History
    Project.*

Within certain geographic regions some quilt patterns seem to become "classics," favored and repeated by a number of generations. In the upstate York County region of South Carolina are found some later examples of the older Whig's Defeat pattern quilts, known locally by the name Richmond Beauty. Emma Hardin Burris (1855–1902) of the Turkey Creek Community, near McConnells, was the maker of a particularly fine and graphic example around 1880. The daughter of William and Mary Caroline Pratt Hardin of Chester County, she was the wife of John T. Burris, a farmer. This quilt is part of the collection of the York County Historic Commission whose Executive Director, Wade B. Fairey, served as a regional coordinator for York County for the South Carolina Quilt History Project.

Plate 3-13.
Double Z or Brown Goose.
90" x 64".
c.1900.
Martha (Mattie) Snowden Emerson Wellnitz (1848–1931).
Made in Cheyenne, Wyoming.
Cotton.
Collection: Wyoming State Museum.
Photo: Wyoming State Museum.
Submitted by the Wyoming State Museum, from their collection (#64.10.394).

Martha Frances (Mattie) Snowden Emerson Wellnitz was born in 1848 in DeKalb County, Missouri, and as a child moved several times with her family. In 1878 on the advice of a friend, she came to Cheyenne, Wyoming, and soon thereafter purchased a dressmaking establishment. At a Baptist prayer meeting she met Elam Solomon Emerson and they were married in 1881. Two children, Paul and Grace, were born to the couple before Elam died in 1885 as a result of an injury suffered during a competition with fellow Union Pacific Railroad workers. To make ends meet, Mattie took in roomers.

Always active, Mattie's son described his mother as "artistic and always busy doing tatting, crocheting, quilting, and beadwork." She was also socially active as a charter member of the Pioneer Club. In 1891 Mattie married Julius Wellnitz, a German immigrant. A few years later Julius was hired as a janitor for the Wyoming State Capitol Building, and the family later occupied living quarters in the basement of the Capitol building. Living essentially isolated at the outskirts of town and in the State House, the Emerson children had an opportunity to meet the state's leading men.

Ever resourceful, Mrs. Wellnitz started serving luncheon to legislators. The walk into town was long and bad weather helped her business. In this way she was able to help Paul financially through Harvard Medical School. When Julius died in 1905, the family left what Paul referred to as "their grand house." Mattie and her daughter Grace lived together until Mattie's death in 1931.

The "Double Z" or "Brown Goose" quilt by Mattie Wellnitz is believed to have been made when she and her family were in residence at the Wyoming Capitol.

Elam Solomon, Paul Waldo, and Martha Frances Emerson. Photo: Courtesy of Wyoming State Museum.

Plate 3-14.
Box Car Quilt – Wild Goose Chase.
60" x 74".
c.1890.
Mary Jane Clubb and family.
Made in Burch, Missouri.
Cotton.
Collection: Arlie M. Razey.
Photo: Richard Walker.
Documented by Quilt Heritage: Washington State.

By the late 1800s the railroad boxcar was the latter-day equivalent of a covered wagon heading west. Instead of taking just a few treasured items that would fit into an ox-drawn wagon, families often hired an entire rail car to ship their belongings. By comparison with other modes, this journey west was short, safe, and relatively comfortable, even though the family often rode in the boxcar with the furniture instead of purchasing expensive coach tickets. The Washington-bound family of Mary Jane and C.H. Clubb of Burch, Missouri, were among those boxcar pioneers lured by the beautiful and high yielding farm properties of the Northwest.

Prior to the journey, "Wild Goose Chase" was made by Mary Jane in about 1890, with the help of all the family women. In all they made 19 quilts. For the boxcar journey the quilts were stacked in piles and basted together to serve as mattresses on the planked floor. When found by the present owner, stacks of quilts were still stitched together.

Mary Jane Clubb and her daughter Etta Clubb.

Plate 3-15.
Pan American Exposition Quilt.
76" x 93".
Top made early 1900s, quilted in 1982.
Mary (Mother of Pearl).
Quilted by Eugenia Mitchell (1903-).
Made in Buffalo, New York and/or Denver, Colorado.
Cotton embroidered block.
Collection: Rocky Mountain Quilt Museum.
Photo: Richard Walker.
Documented by the Colorado Quilting Council, Inc. and submitted by The Rocky Mountain Quilt Museum.

The Pan American Exposition held in Buffalo, New York, in 1901 was designed to show the progress of the century in the New World. At a cost of almost $2.5 million, its theme was the promotion of commerce and it presented a picture of the possibilities of modern electricity. The exposition's New York State Building, an imitation of the Greek Parthenon, survives to house the Buffalo and Erie County Historical Society.

What people remember most, however, about the Pan American Exposition is that United States President William McKinley, in Buffalo to present a trade speech in the Temple of Music Building, was shot on September 6, 1901. He died from infection a few days later, and the exposition's opening was postponed.

A number of quilts have surfaced which reflect the theme of the exposition and include blocks of the exposition buildings and the "Martyred President," as well as his successor Theodore Roosevelt, and both of their wives. Also featured were King Edward of England and Germany's Emperor William (Wilhelm). An unknown stitcher named Mary made this turkey red embroidered top. Her outline-embroidered blocks included not only a myriad of the exposition buildings, including a "House Upside Down," Wild Water Sports, Barnes' Diving Elks, and the Electric Tower, but also more traditional renditions of flowers, animals, and children. She included her daughter Pearl's name. Even though the family's last name is unknown, we do know that mother and daughter moved from Buffalo, New York, to Denver, Colorado, in 1905, in hopes that the western climate would help Pearl recover from tuberculosis. The move must have been beneficial since Pearl married and lived until 1980. The top was donated to St. Johns in the Wilderness Episcopal Church and subsequently purchased and quilted in 1982 by Eugenia Hartmeister Mitchell. The quilt resides in the Rocky Mountain Quilt Museum in Golden, Colorado, part of Ms. Mitchell's original donation of 100 quilts to that facility.

The Rocky Mountain Quilt Museum, incorporated in 1981, was Eugenia Hartmeister Mitchell's dream. Born in 1903 in Brazil, where her parents John and Theodora Mueller Hartmeister were Lutheran missionaries, Eugenia grew up in Storm Lake, Iowa. There she learned to quilt from her mother in spite of a keener interest in active, "tomboy" activites. Over many years she purchased quilts and quilt tops. Her desire was that her collection be both perserved and seen by the public, a wish fulfilled when the museum opened in 1990 in Golden, Colorado.

Plate 3-16.
Flying Geese.
69" x 73".
c.1914.
Johanna (Hanna) Schmidt Sterns (1859-1940).
Made in Russell Gulch, Colorado.
Wool.
Collection: Edna Mae Miller.
Photo: Richard Walker.
Documented by the Montana Heritage Quilt
   Project.

A practical, sturdy suggan or cowboy quilt, made to be used in a bedroll was created in the Colorado mining camp of Russell Gulch by Johanna (Hanna) Schmidt Sterns (1859–1940), the daughter of an immigrant tailor from Prussia. She chose plain weave woolens in dark hues to piece the quilt. She tied it with red and black wool yarn and used a wool batting wrapped in cheesecloth. The quilt has a gray striped cotton backing.

While in the camp Johanna Sterns also pieced an elegant Pineapple quilt of the finest colored taffetas and red sateen, in sharp contrast to the rough cowboy quilt. Her daughter Bertha's dressmaking business included sewing for "the ladies of the night" who could afford the best for their dresses. That quilt was made from those scraps. Like most quiltmakers Johanna made fancy as well as plain quilts, the one for necessity, the other to satisfy the wish to make something fine and decorative. Both quilts were brought by Johanna's daughter Bertha Miller to homestead in the Sarpy Creek area of Big Horn County, Montana.

Scene from a cowboy camp.
Photo: Courtesy of Colorado Historical Society.

Plate 3-17.
Star of Bethlehem.
76" x 91".
c.1920.
Margaret (or Anna) David.
Made in Peshawbestown, Michigan.
Cotton fabric with cotton filling.
Collection: Michigan State University Museum.
Photo: Peter Glendinning.
Documented by the Michigan Quilt Project.

A Star Of Bethlehem quilt was made about 1920 by Margaret or Anna David of the Odawa in Peshawbestown on the Leelenau Peninsula (MI). This particular quilt is a good example of the style of quilt favored by Native American quiltmakers in Michigan during this time periods. The floral motifs that surround the star are adapted from earlier bead and quillwork of the Woodlands Indians.

In spite of concerted efforts, some state documentation projects experienced difficulty in eliciting minority-made quilts and their studies therefore did not accurately reflect the numbers and varieties of quilts being produced by these communities. In some places follow-up studies are remedying this situation.

Plate 3-18.
Masonic Emblem Quilt.
94" x 94".
c.1849.
J.T. Freeland and Sarah Culbertson Freeland.
Made in Freelandville, Indiana.
Cotton.
Collection: Indiana State Museum. (#71.968.59.1).
Photo: Indiana State Museum.
Documented by the Indiana Quilt Registry Project.

Sarah Culbertson Freeland of Freelandville, Knox County, Indiana, worked on a quilt for her husband J.T. Freeland over a four- or five-year period. Freeland, a physician, was Master Mason of the Vincennes Commandary. The quilt made for him in the late 1840s by his second wife includes a central medallion with the Masonic emblem, various floras, and symbols associated with the fraternal organization such as a mallet, chisel, trowel, and crossed keys. Freemasonry was a social and charitable organization brought to the United States in the early decades of the eighteenth century. This quilt was so important to the family that in later years they recorded its history in one corner with a laundry marking pen.

Plate 3-19.
Prairie Star.
70" x 89".
c.1870.
Narcissa Mayo Cooper (1848–1925).
Made in Camden, Alabama.
Cotton.
Collection: Daniel Brooks.
Photo: Harold Kilgore.
Documented by the Alabama Quilt Search Project.

The 1925 obituary of Narcissa Mayo Cooper (1848–1925) described her as one of Camden, Alabama's "most esteemed and useful." The daughter of seven-foot-tall butcher and carpenter William Mayo and his wife Martha Ridgell, Narcissa was a lifelong resident of Camden. An 1866 graduate of the Wilcox Female Institute, she was described as "a teacher of wonderful ability" who "influenced the lives of many young people for that which is good." Narcissa was also an excellent seamstress and taught sewing along with academic subjects. Her Confederate veteran husband Frederick Cooper (1837–1923), New York-born but Alabama-raised, was a wheelwright and a cabinetmaker and undertaker, occupations often conjoined. Although this hardworking couple had no children of their own, Frederick's niece and her three children, Fred, Arthur, and Narcissa Logue, made their home with them for many years.

A collection of well-made quilts by Narcissa Mayo Cooper remains intact, along with her sewing basket. Some of her quilts were made in the English tradition, influenced by contact with her husband's parents, who were from England. Among the items in the collection are this "Prairie Star" quilt, two coverlets, one of her mother's quilts, and a quilt made by Frederick's niece, Sally Sheffield Logue.

Narcissa Mayo Cooper's "Prairie Star" quilt is typical of many of those made by her – strong visually, simply quilted, and made of a variety of fabrics. Furniture, tools, photographs, letters, and needlework remain as testament to the Coopers' lifestyle and industrious activity, along with the diaries kept for 62 years, first by Frederick, and after his death, by Narcissa.

Narcissa Mayo Cooper (1848–1925).

Plate 3-20.
Mariner's Compass.
91" x 92".
c.1840.
Mary A. Beers (early 1800s).
Made in Stratford, Connecticut.
Calico and muslin.
Collection: Stratford Historical Society.
Photo: Richard Walker.
Documented by the Connecticut Quilt Search Project.

"A miracle of fine needlework" were words used by a 1910 Bridgeport Connecticut newspaper to describe the Mariner's Compass quilt that had been made in the previous century by Miss Mary A. Beers of Stratford. The quilt was so recognized while exhibited amongst 80 historic bed quilts at the Stratford Congregational Church Parish House.

The quilt received special attention because earlier in the year it had won a $100 first prize award in a national contest sponsored by Goodin, Reid & Co. of Cincinnati, Ohio, the manufacturer of Reddisode cotton batts. The contest, known as the Reddisode Revolutionary Quilt Contest, was conducted through local department stores, which forwarded regional winners to the national competition. The Howland Dry Goods Company of Bridgeport received 103 entries and selected three finalists. They related that "it was not an easy task that confronted the judges." All entries were exhibited in the store; the three accepted for competition in the window, the rest in the "spacious Carpet Hall on the third floor." In promoting the display The Howland Dry Goods Company promised that "every woman interested in quilting and in nice needlework will be repaid for the time spent at the exhibit."

The quilt contest was entered by Mrs. Otis B. Curtis, who submitted the quilt made by Mary A. Beers. Her quilt was one of the entries representing Howland Dry Goods, and it won first prize over the second place winner, Mrs. Morgan, representing Seattle's Bon Marche. Third place went to Mrs. Alex McIntosh of Decatur, Illinois, sponsored by Lin & Scruggs. In all, 30 cash prizes were awarded by Goodin, Reid & Co.

Walter S. Curtis was described in the newspaper article as owner of the quilt, Mary A. Beers as his great-aunt. Silas Beers, Mary's father, had been a drummer in the Revolutionary War, a member of the 5th Regiment from Connecticut. He also served in the War of 1812. The lovely red, green, and yellow quilt with running vine quilting stitches was eventually presented to the Stratford Historical Society by the Curtis/s Society, a family geneological society.

Plate 3-21.
Yo-Yo Quilt.
82" x 98".
c.1941.
Myra P. Hilliker (1867-1945).
Made in Pioche, Nevada.
Cotton.
Collection: Bette G. Cole.
Photo: Richard Walker.
Documented by the Nevada State Heritage Quilt Project. (PCP22)

Another name for a Yo-Yo quilt is Bed of Roses. Perhaps Myra P. Hilliker had this name in mind in 1938 and 1939 when she spent most of her time on the Woodworth Ranch in Hamblin Valley near Pioche, Nevada, outside under a tree where she had her bed. She worked on the quilt for at least an hour a day for an entire year.

Myra was born in Nevada in 1867. She had been married to a Mr. Green and they owned a carnival that traveled the Union Pacific Railway lines with five or six cars of amusements and rides. Myra became the carnival fortune teller, reading palms, cards, tea leaves, and a crystal ball. Her carnival skirts would become one source of fabrics for her Yo-Yo quilt. When Mr. Green tired of the carnival and the crowds, he sold the business and became postmaster of the 50-resident town of Modena, Utah, a railroad water stop for the old steam engines. When Mr. Green died, Myra went to live with a sister in California, where she married Arthur Hilliker. After her sister died and the couple separated, Myra came back to Pioche to live with a niece. The niece's husband did not want her there and refused to let her in the house when he was home. At such times Myra sat outside under the tree, and that's where she pieced her Bed of Roses quilt.

Myra later moved into town and she and Art resumed their marriage. He cared for her very lovingly until her death in 1944. Art sold the quilt to her neighbor Bette G. Cole to help pay for Myra's burial. This was in keeping with Myra's request since this neighbor had often visited and run errands for her. Because of the Nevada State Heritage Quilt Project, Myra's story is told.

Myra and Arthur Hilliker.

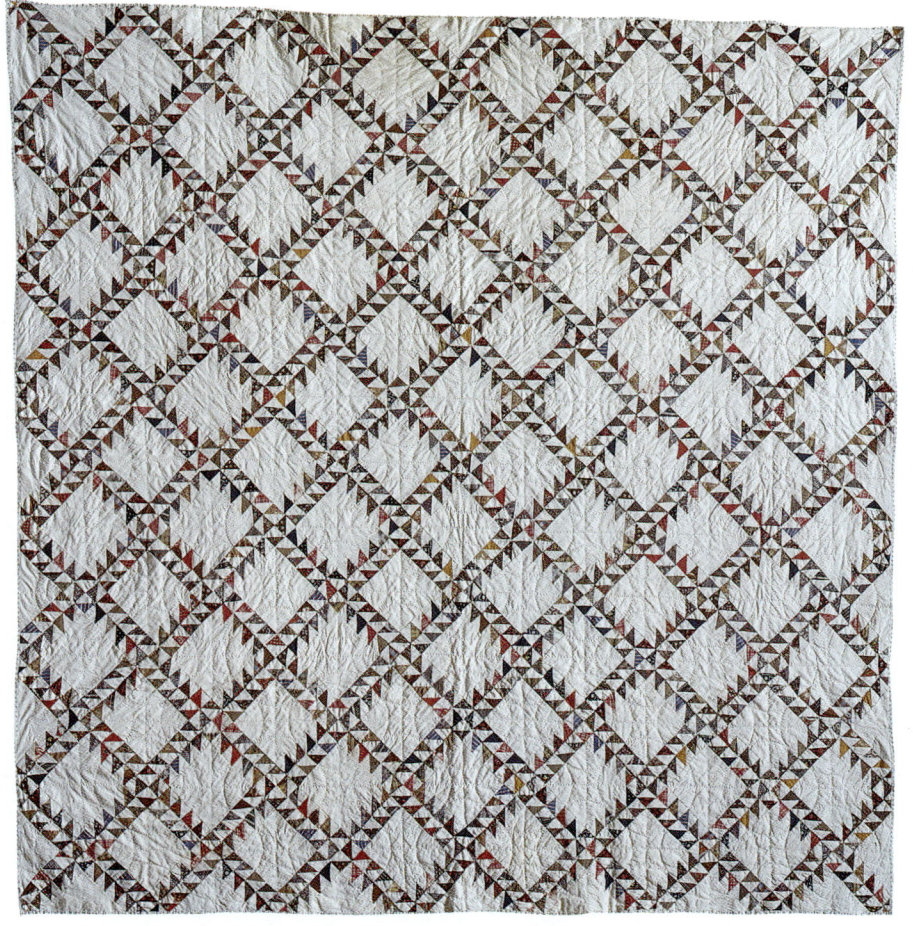

Plate 3-22.
Sawtooth Square Variation.
77" x 75".
c.1870-1890
Hannah M. Cressy (1824–1905).
Made in South Londonderry, Vermont.
Cotton.
Collection: Rex and Phyllis Doane.
Photo: Ken Burris, Shelburne, Vermont, courtesy of the Vermont Quiltsearch.
Documented by the Vermont Quiltsearch (#2912).

The Cressy house at Winhall Station, Londonderry, VT.

Hannah Cressy did not allow blindness to stop her quiltmaking. Hannah cut the pieces for her patchwork, using a cardboard template. Members of her family would string similar colors together on a thread, and place them in her sewing box. This way Hannah could distinguish the light colors from the dark. Her quilt, with its hundreds of sawtooth triangles made between 1870 and 1890, is testament to how she prevented her disability from impeding productivity.

Born in 1824 in Jamaica, Vermont, to Alpheus and Lydia Cressy, both Hannah and her brother George lost their sight as youths because of an inherited disease. The brother and sister made their home together in South Londonderry, Vermont. Both died in 1905, just four months apart. A niece later placed Hannah's quilt for sale in a local antique shop. A great-nephew, Rex Doane, wanted the quilt to stay in the family so he bought it. He's convinced that Hannah would be both amazed and pleased at the attention her quilt has received.

Hannah M. Cressy and her brother, George Cressy.

Plate 3-23.
Slave Chain.
67" x 82".
c.1930.
Phoeba Johnson (1883–1983).
Made in Wilkinson County, Mississippi.
Cottons.
Collection: Mississippi State Historical Museum (#85.53.2).
Photo: Mississippi Department of Archives and History.
Documented and submitted by the Mississippi State Historical Museum.

Phoeba Johnson (1883–1983) was just seven or eight years old when she pieced her first quilt, "a little nine-patch." She proudly remembered her father making a big fuss over her for that accomplishment. This Wilkinson County (MS) native went on to make many quilts in her long lifetime. From her grandmother Thomsie, a former slave brought from Virginia to Mississippi, she learned how to make what she calls the Slave Chain pattern.

In an interview with Mississippi folklife researcher Roland Freeman, Mrs. Johnson, then well into her nineties, explained that she no longer quilted because her hands could no longer take it. "But," she added, "I can still piece up one of the prettiest spreads around."[8] Two of her daughters, Annie Dennis of Mississippi and Emma Russell of Louisiana, have carried on their mother's quilting tradition.

Mrs. Phoeba Johnson (1883–1983).
Photo ©Roland Freeman.

Plate 3-24.
Flower Basket Appliqué Quilt.
64" x 80".
1840-1860.
Eliza Hicks.
Made in New York State.
Cotton.
Collection: Margaret Thurston Carroll.
Photo: Richard Walker.
Documented by the Iowa Quilt Research Project (#Q43).

Becoming the new wife of a recent widower is never an easy task, especially when the late wife has been accomplished. Such was probably the case for Lucy Ferry Jones McLaughlin Desmond (1848–1928). Tired of the attention a Flower Basket appliqué quilt by her husband's first wife, Eliza Hicks, was receiving, in a fit of jealousy, Lucy began to rip off the flower appliqués. Her excuse was that she needed the muslin for a bed sheet. The family stopped her and put the quilt away. It was never again used.

Born in New York State, Lucy moved as a young child to Wisconsin with her parents. She grew up without knowing her father and was raised by several uncles. At 18 she moved to Burr Oak (IA) and married Joseph McLaughlin. She had two young children when Joseph died of scarlet fever. She then married Mr. Desmond who had recently been widowed. The quilt was among his late wife's possessions. This quilt and its story have been carefully passed from generation to generation and now belong to Lucy's great-granddaughter, who was ten when Lucy died and remembers her well. To this day the quilt is still missing some of the original appliqué pieces.

Lucy Ferry Jones McLaughlin Desmond (1848–1928).

Plate 3-25.
French Smoothing Iron.
60" x 78".
c.1903.
Mary McCollough Maxwell (1867–1946).
Made in Liberty, Arkansas.
Collection: Ollie Sugg.
Photo: Rogers Historical Museum.
Documented by the Stitches in Time: A Legacy of Ozark Quilts project, a survey conducted by the Rogers Historical Museum.

At age 19, a time when Mary McCollough (1867–1946) of Carroll County, Arkansas might have been thinking about courtship and marriage, her mother died leaving 11 younger brothers and sisters. The youngest was just 18 months old. Mary assumed the burden of caring for her siblings. Only after that youngest brother turned 18 did she wed Joel Maxwell. Maxwell had left Liberty, Arkansas, to work as a cowboy. He returned to the Ozarks "full of tales" but ready to buy a 104 acre farm. Mary McCollough could see that he was a hard worker.

To celebrate her 1903 wedding, Mary pieced a French Smoothing Iron pattern quilt. To get enough cloth, she sewed for neighbors in exchange for enough fabric scraps to make a block. She raised her own cotton for batting in a little patch in her yard and carded it herself. In later years her five children would recall picking out cotton seeds by hand so the fibers could be prepared for batts. Mary made many quilts over the years, an avocation carried on by her daughter, Ollie Sugg, the owner of this quilt.

Joel and Mary McCollough Maxwell.

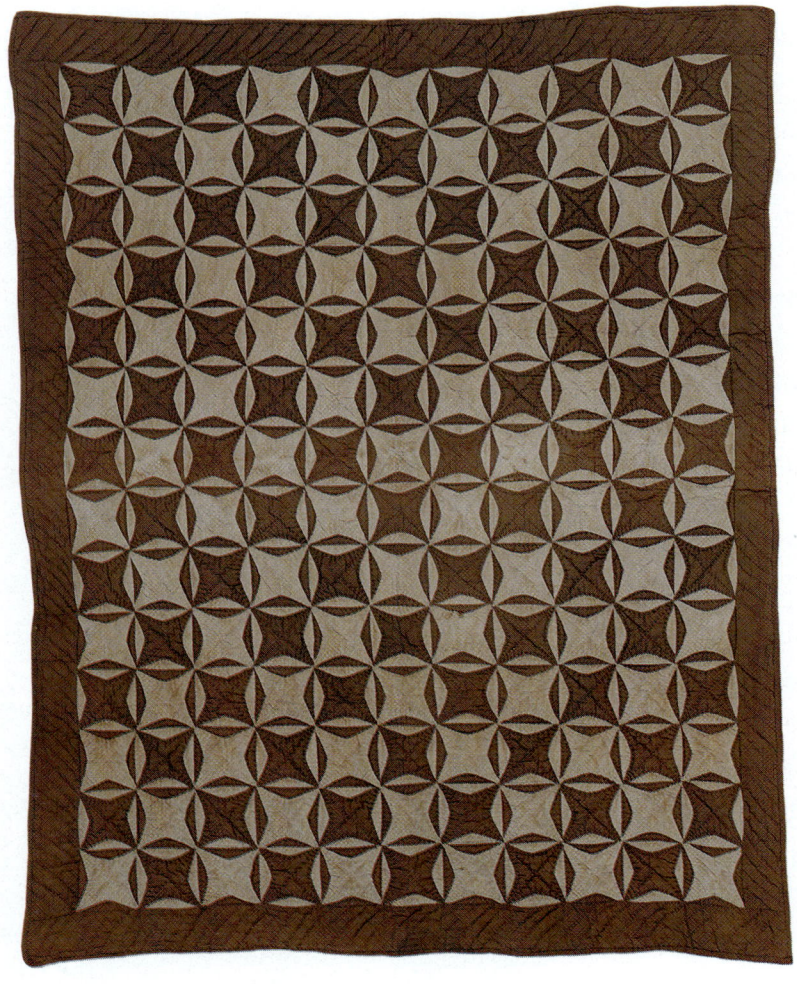

Plate 3-26.
Orange Peel Crib Quilt.
39" x 49".
1895-1900.
Lilla Owens Thrash (1877–1964).
Made in La Grange, Troup County, Georgia.
Cotton.
Collection: Mary Davis.
Photo: Richard Walker.
Documented by the Georgia Quilt Project (#2194).

A heartbreaking story spread through the room at an August 1990 quilt day held in Columbus, Georgia; the story was so sad that each volunteer felt compelled to share it with the next. Everyone gathered around and discussed it.

The dialogue concerned a green and white Orange Peel quilt, crib sized, made for a child. Its maker, Lilla Owens Thrash (1877–1964) of Troup County (GA), daughter of J.P. and Sally Scogin Owens, had learned to quilt with her family. Married to George Thrash, a farmer, she had made the crib quilt when she was just 18, in anticipation of the birth of her first child. That baby – and three successive ones – each lived only 24 to 48 hours after birth. The quilt would never be needed for any of Lilla's babies.

Over the years Lilla made many other quilts, including one for the wedding of her niece, who is the caretaker of the little quilt that carried so much hope.

George Thrash, Lilla Owens Thrash, and nephews. The photo was take by Lilla's brother, a professional photographer.

Plate 3-27.
Whitework Quilt.
96" x 98".
1850.
Frances Mooney Smith.
Made in Ashland, New Hampshire.
Cotton.
Collection: Ashland Historic Society.
Photo: Richard Walker.
Documented by the New Hampshire Quilt Documentation Project (HSA 784).

Recent quilt studies have indicated that quilts with corners cut out for four poster beds usually have their origins in New England. This beautiful white whole-cloth quilt with exquisite workmanship is a fine example. Made for the wedding of Frances Mooney Smith, this quilt hails from Ashland, New Hampshire. The designer of the quilting pattern was Sarah Dana, daughter of a local Ashland doctor. The medallion motif includes a six sectioned scalloped feather circle surrounded by leaves, flowers, and grapes. Neighbors joined in helping quilt this bridal masterpiece.

Frances was married in 1855. A young woman of considerable wealth, she even had personalized music books with leather covers.

Plate 3-28.
Little Red Schoolhouse.
66" x 85".
c.1920.
Margaret Fay Garrity (1868–1956).
Made in Denver, Colorado.
Cotton, cotton embroidery thread, muslin cotton backing.
Collection: Rocky Mountain Quilt Museum (#1991.1.10).
Photo: Richard Walker.
Documented by the Colorado Quilting Council, Inc. and submitted by the Rocky Mountain Quilt Museum.

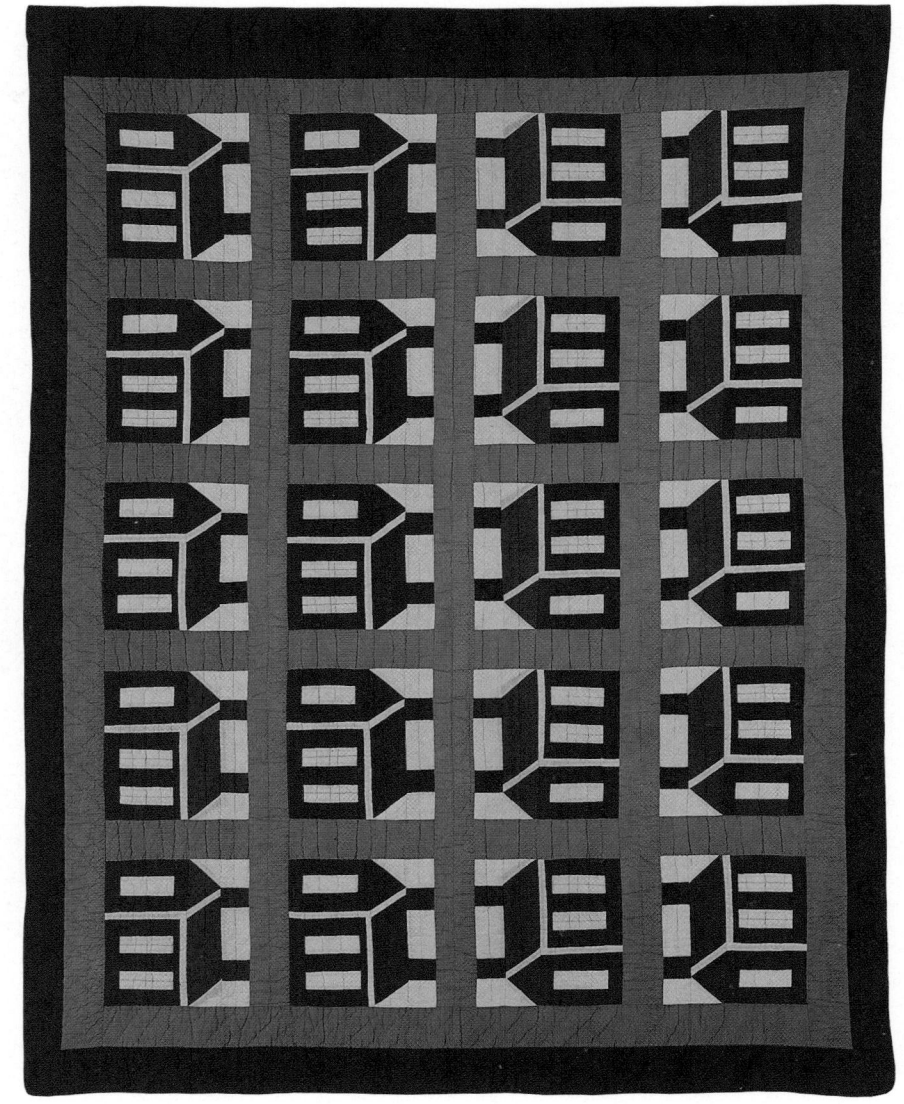

Margaret Fay Garrity (1868–1956) was born in Middletown, New York, but moved to Denver, Colorado, with her family in 1881. After the death of her husband, she made her home with relatives, typically living with each one for three or four months at a time, and then moving on. In an effort to repay them for their hospitality, she would sometimes make them a quilt.

The "Little Red Schoolhouse" quilt was given to a niece, Ruth Jennings Hanson, in 1926, who then passed it on to her daughter, Marjorie Hanson Sweeney. The quilt was subsequently traded to Eugenia Mitchell, who donated it to the Rocky Mountain Quilt Museum in 1991. The simple, graphic, Schoolhouse pattern has remained popular for decades.

Plate 3-29
Schoolhouse.
82" x 85".
1935.
Bertha Abbott and Lula Abbott.
Made in Lima, Allen County, Ohio.
Cotton.
Collection: Allen County Historical Society (#0616.0036).
Photo: Richard Walker.
Documented by the Ohio Quilt Research Project (#ACH 52.1).

An interesting but unrealistic depression era scheme to assist older citizens who had lost savings was launched by Long Beach, California, retired physician Francis E. Townsend, whose own savings had been wiped out. Like a gaunt Pied Piper, he made emotional and political appeals claiming it was the "right" of every "senior citizen" age 60 or over to receive an income of 200 dollars a month, provided he or she spent that sum within the month. The plan was to be administered by the federal government and supported by sales or gross income taxes.

Townsend attracted the support of many senior citizens who formed "Townsend Clubs." In Allen County, Ohio, Clubs #1 and #2 of Lima attempted to raise funds by making a raffle quilt. Miss Bertha Abbott pieced the Schoolhouse quilt, Miss Lula Abbott embroidered the names in turkey red thread, and Mrs. Sarah Voltz sold raffle tickets. In all, the club raised $111.60 for the cause.[9]

Fundraising quilts are found throughout American quilting history, and were particularly popular during the late nineteenth and early twentieth centuries. Their inscriptions and signatures are often valuable records of places and events.

Townsend Club Quilt / Makers, 1935. L to R: Miss Bertha Abbot, Miss Lula Abbott, Mrs. Sarah Voltz.
Photo courtesy Allen County Historical Society.

Plate 3-30.
Blue and White Scrap Quilt.
64" x 84".
c.1925-1935.
Azelie Maillet Girouard (1881–1972).
Made in New Bedford, Massachusetts.
Cotton, cotton batting.
Collection: Jane Barnhart.
Photo: Richard Walker.
Documented by the Medfield, Massachusetts Quilt Documentation, to be incorporated in MASS Quilts: The Massachusetts Quilt Documentation Project.

Azelie Maillet Girouard (1881–1972)
Photo courtesy of Jane Barnhart.

When he knew he was gravely ill, Augustin Girouard advised his wife to move to New Bedford, Massachusetts, with their 12 children so that the family could find good employment opportunities. From their farm home in Buctouche, New Brunswick, Canada, his widow, Azelie Maillet Girouard, sent the oldest girls, Hermine and Roberta, as scouts to New Bedford. They found work, rented a house, bought furniture on time, and sent for the rest of the family. At age 45, Azelie Girouard (1881–1972) uprooted and moved.

From the packages of factory cutaways brought home by family members working in various mills, Azelie made quilts. A blue and white scrap quilt has been the object of much curiosity for her granddaughter, Jane Barnhart. Through interviews with the family she has been able to trace the origins of the fabrics. She reports that the quilt "is clearly made from cuts from a dress factory and there are several prints [in] two or three colorways, same print, different colors." Although it is uncertain from which exact factory in New Bedford they came, these fabrics were brought home by Azelie's son Aurele, who worked as a sewing machine repairman in the local sewing shops. Jane's Aunt Omerine remembers little bundles of fabrics in different shapes stored in the attic.

Jane adds that some of the "plain blue fabrics in this quilt are cotton shirting fabrics, probably from Macy Shirt Company, where my mother's older sisters, Jeanne and Bertha, worked." The denser white sheeting was probably contributed by Bertha's fiancé "Donat Boisvert, who worked as a loom fixer at [the] Nashawena Mill, the Hathaway Mills, and the Wamsutta Mills, where this type of fabric was woven and finished."

Azelie machine pieced and machine appliquéd this quilt top made from factory scraps sometime during the late 1920s or early 1930s. It was one of many made during those years. She used a heavy cotton batting and flour sacks for backing. She had learned never to waste anything. In Canada she had raised sheep, sheared the wool, carded and spun the yarn, and woven it into blankets. She knitted wool underwear, made clothes for the family, and hooked hundreds of rugs from rags. A highlight in her years of home sewing was when her Singer treadle machine was converted to electricity.

Granddaughter Jane's detective work on fabrics and style of craftsmanship enabled her to also attribute to Azelie a quilt owned by one of her aunts. This overjoyed her aunt, who had not realized that she actually possessed one of the quilts that had been made by her mother. This aunt of Jane's had fond memories of playing around Azelie Girouard's quilting frame as a youngster.

Plate 3-31.
Arizona Commemorative.
57" x 71".
1938.
Emma Andres (1902–1987).
Made in Prescott, Arizona.
Cottons.
Collection: Mark and Jill Tetreau.
Photo: Richard Walker.
Documented by the Arizona Quilt Project (#P118).

Emma Andres beside the last quilt she made. Clipping from the PRESCOTT CAREER *newspaper, 1976.*

Emma Andres grew up in Prescott, Arizona, born in 1902 before the territory became a state. Her father was in the tobacco business and made cigars which he peddled by pack animal. He opened a cigar store and of the five Andres children, it was Emma who helped run it. Life in the cigar store became especially sweet for her when her father added a line of newspapers and magazines to the store's inventory. As Emma read them by the hour, her narrow rural world suddenly broadened. In magazines and newspapers she found people and ideas. It was from a periodical that Emma sent for the quilt kit that would become the first of her many quilts.

In newspapers Emma read stories of other quilters and started corresponding with a number of them, including Carrie Hall of Leavenworth, Kansas, author of *Romance of the Patchwork Quilt*; Charles Pratt of Philadelphia; and New Jersey historian Florence Peto. She savored these people's letters, advice, encouragement, and other quilt talk. Her pen relationships lasted for years, and each letter was carefully preserved in a scrapbook.

In fact, Emma kept just about everything. Inside a candy box were colored fabric swatches held in individual match boxes. A collection of needles labeled and kept as souvenirs of projects and an assemblage of thimbles used by her friends were among her treasures. Eventually the cigar store became Emma's Happiness Museum, where this town character displayed her quilts and those of others.

In 1984 Emma Andres received Arizona's first Quilt Artisan Award and was named the state's Quilter of the Year. This talented quiltmaker is remembered in her later years for her hats and long dresses. The Sharlott Hall Museum in Prescott, Arizona, mounted an exhibit of her quilts and almost every day for her last three years she would walk down from her rest home and talk with the public about her quilts. For the aging Emma, this was a comforting substitute for the former cigar store museum.[10] She died in 1987, leaving a legacy in both quilts and priceless memorabilia. The "Arizona Commemorative" quilt was made in 1938 and is an original design.

Mark and Jill Tetreau, quilt owners with their daughters Kali and Amber and the family pet Hama.

Plate 3-32.
Friendship Quilt.
68" x 82".
c.1924.
Elsie Allred Bland and the Help One Another Club
Made in Rocky Branch, Arkansas, now under the waters of Beaver Lake.
Muslin.
Collection: Ruth Bland.
Photo: Rogers Historical Museum.
Documented by the Stitches in Time: A Legacy of Ozark Quilts project, a survey conducted by the Rogers Historical Museum.

Beaver Lake now covers the site of the little town of Rocky Branch, Arkansas. For Elsie Allred Bland, a lasting memento of the town was her embroidered "Friendship Quilt" made about 1924, a memento of the Help One Another Club, a neighborhood woman's club she had founded.

Elsie provided the muslin from Stroud's store in nearby Rogers (AR), and members worked on blocks at their monthly meetings. Elsie ended up making eight of the blocks, including ones for her mother Martha Susan Allred, mother-in-law Mary Bland, and sister Lela Allred.

In 1940, before the new dam had been completed, Elsie left Rocky Branch for Rogers (AR). There she started a new group, the Aim High Club, but memories of the old community lived on, tangibly reinforced by the friends' commemorative effort.

Elsie Allred Bland, c.1960.
Photo: courtesy of Richard Bland.

Plate 3-33.
Chester Dare Crazy Quilt.
80" x 88".
c.1882.
Anna Hines Miller (Mrs. Luther J. Miller)
     (1857–1897).
Made in Warren County, Kentucky.
Wool, velvet border.
Collection: Western Kentucky Museum
     (#1983.7.1)
Photo: Richard Walker.
Documented by the Kentucky Quilt Project, Inc.

Perhaps no quilt represents the famous Bluegrass region of Kentucky better than a crazy quilt that includes the portrait of the beautiful saddle horse, Chester Dare (1882–1904). Mary Washington Clarke in her book, *Kentucky Quilts and Their Makers* describes the quilt as full of "Bluegrass pride in an equine tradition, local flora and fauna, and romantic legends."[11]

The horse himself had an interesting history. Bred by J.W. Garrett of Versailles (KY), of Nannie Garrett and Black Squirrel 58, in 1882 the three-day-old colt was purchased by J.C. Graves. Garrett, not wanting to sell him, had named a price he was sure would be refused. At the time of the purchase the new owner's wife was reading the story "Zilpah" with its young hero named Chester Dare, so she selected that for the colt's name.[12]

The 15.3-hand mahogany bay stallion started to attract attention when as a three-year-old he won his classes at Lexington and other Kentucky fairs. He had a graceful and impressive appearance and became an almost unbeatable contender. He was considered smart and had a good disposition.

The quiltmaker, Annie Hines Miller (1857–1897), is said to have in the early 1880s started this intricate parlor throw of smooth wools, fine textured cottons, and ornamental stitching. Over the years she added flowers, birds, and animals in embroidery and added her own signature. Near the center she appliquéd a portrait of Chester Dare. Family legend tells that hairs from the horse's tail were carried by riverboat to New Orleans so a piece of matching velvet could be purchased for the portrait.

Further legend has it that the young woman was guarded jealously by an older husband who tried to keep her at home. It is said that when he left home he would take her shoes so that she would not be able to leave.

Perhaps she worked on her quilt during those confining moments. Her death is said to have occurred from pneumonia after walking shoeless through the snow to her mother's neighboring farm. This quilt is now part of the collection of The Kentucky Museum at Western Kentucky University in Bowling Green (KY).

Drawing of Chester Dare from Famous Saddle Horses *by Emily Ellen Scharf.*

Plate 3-34.
Wool Nine-Patch.
67" x 79".
c.1950.
Maker of outer quilt: Kate Smith Heslop Heim.
Maker of inner quilt unknown.
Outer quilt made in Benton, Wisconsin.
Wool, silk, rayon.
Collection: Jean Weness.
Photo: Richard Walker.
Documented by the Minnesota Quilt Project (MNQP#WF080).

Examples of quilters' frugality, of their resurrecting old quilts by using them as fillers for new quilts, fascinated Minnesota Quilt Project co-chair Norm Steere. At a Quilt Discovery Day in Worthington in July 1988, two such quilt-within-a-quilts appeared.

One was a large-scale wool Nine-Patch that Kate Smith Heslop created c.1950 in Benton, Wisconsin, to cover a worn Square-in-a-Square pattern quilt, also made of mostly wool, probably during the last quarter of the nineteenth century. The old quilt had been given to her by her "rich" friend Alma Latham. Kate attached the new top along the edges, covering just the front. The quilt back was still in good shape so it didn't need to be covered and its fine quilting and piecing reminded Kate of "strippy" quilts from her family's home in County Durham, England. Over the years she had made her home in Benton, Wisconsin, and Minneapolis, Minnesota. Many families in this mining area had come from the same area of England. The quilt came with her when she moved to Austin (MN) to live with her daughter, Daisy Grundy. Kate died in 1975 at the age of 92.

Since the second cover had only been tied, the present quiltowner, Kate's granddaughter Jean Weness, agreed to open some of the ties so the older, inner quilt could be assessed by the Minnesota Quilt Project.

Kate Smith Heslop with grandchildren: (LtoR) Margaret, Bob, Katy, and Jean Grundy, c.1950.

Plate 3-35.
Grandmother's Flower Garden Quilt.
46" x 56".
c.1865.
Hanson Penn Diltz
Quilted by Carrie Diltz Elgin & Elizabeth Diltz Cushman.
Made in Cynthiana, Kentucky.
Silk.
Collection: Kentucky Historical Society (#80.28.1)
Photo: Kentucky Historical Society.
Documented by the Kentucky Quilt Project, Inc.

In the waning years of the Civil War, nine-year-old Hanson Penn Diltz of Cynthiana, Kentucky, sewed together the pieces of a hexagonal Flower Garden quilt top. His template was a six-sided shape of tin about the size of a dime.

At a later date Hanson's sisters, Carrie Diltz Elgin and Elizabeth Diltz Cushman, completed his quilt as a mosaic parlor throw with a scarlet silk border. An embroidered "D" appears in three corners and the date 1907 in the fourth. Today this quilt is in the collection of the Kentucky Historical Society.

Plate 3-36.
Printed Flannel Flag Quilt.
69" x 67".
Date unknown.
Maria Fogg Manchester (1855–1933).
Made in Mascoma, New Hampshire.
Wool, cotton backing, cotton embroidery.
Collection: Private.
Photo: Courtsey of owner.
Documented by the New Hampshire Quilt Documentation Project (#BML347).

A two sided quilt of dark heavy wools and flannels was made in New Hampshire by Maria Fogg Manchester. Married to George Washington Manchester, she was a farm wife in Mascoma. Born in Bristol in 1855, she was of English and American Indian ancestry. Maria died in Mascoma in 1933 and her quilt remained on the family farm, eventually passing onto her great-granddaughter.

On one side of the quilt the pieces are wools, cut in various size rectangles. Herringbone stitches in cotton embroidery thread surround each piece. The other side was made by joining colorful printed cigar flannels, the kind popular during the first quarter of the twentieth century and given as premiums by tobacco manufacturers.

Back of "Printed Flannel Flag Quilt."

Plate 3-37.
Feather Plumes with Coxcombs.
70" x 75".
c.1890.
Cora Viola Howell Slaughter (1860-1941) and
Edith Stowe (–1938).
Made in Cochise County, Arizona.
Cotton.
Collection: Arizona Historical Society.
Photo: Richard Walker.
Documented by the Arizona Quilt Project.

Cora Viola Howell (1860–1941) was just 18 in 1879 when she met John Slaughter, nearly 20 years her senior, in New Mexico. The Howell family, formerly of Missouri, had lived briefly in Montana, Utah, and Nevada and were on their way to Texas when the chance meeting took place. Slaughter was a widower with two small children and was in New Mexico awaiting the arrival of his cattle from Texas. A former Confederate soldier and Texas Ranger, he had earned a reputation as the tough sheriff from Tombstone, Arizona. The Howells were persuaded to join Slaughter so they combined cattle herds and all set out for Arizona. Viola rode alongside Mr. Slaughter and wrote in her memoires that "it was love at first sight." In spite of her mother's objections, Viola married him enroute to Arizona.

There, John Slaughter began a wholesale and retail meat business. Viola joined her husband on cattle drives, though she was terrified of Indians. In 1884 the couple bought the 65,000-acre San Bernardino Ranch along the Mexican border, which had been deserted for more than 50 years because of Apache raids. They also kept a home in Tombstone so the two children could attend school, but they had to give it up when cattle prices dropped. After they moved full-time to the ranch, it began to prosper. They built a large home there with fine furnishings, and they even took in foster children. The ranch became a self-contained extended family compound. As the family had domestic help, Viola found time for needlework. With her friend Edith Stowe, she created this fine quilt, a Feather Plume and Coxcomb appliqué. The Slaughters left the ranch in 1921 and moved to the town of Douglas. San Bernadino Ranch is presently a National Historic Landmark.[13]

Plate 3-38.
Miracle Quilt of Democracy.
66" x 84".
c.1932.
Catherine Elizabeth (Kate) Waldron McClenny
 (1868–1952).
Made in Jacksonville Beach, Florida.
Cotton and wool.
Collection: Beaches Area Historical Society.
Photo: Richard Walker.
Documented by the Florida Quilt Heritage Project.

Certainly the political campaign of Franklin Delano Roosevelt for becoming the 32nd United States president generated strong anticipation and hope for the future. For Catherine Elizabeth (Kate) Waldron McClenny, a woman in her sixties who had always been interested in politics, this campaign inspired a first quilting effort.

Known as the "Miracle Quilt of Democracy," this quilt was Kate's original design and features Roosevelt's Little White House, the Warm Springs, Georgia cottage he built as a retreat. According to a 1950 Jacksonville newspaper story, this small house symbolized the social security movement. The anchor commemorates Roosevelt's 1913–21 tenure with the United States Navy Department.

Other designs include Rose of Sharon, lilies of the valley, a donkey, a lamb, and a dove. An oxcart symbolizes the pioneers, and the border features a highway complete with a team of horses, an automobile, and an airplane. Kate described her quilt as being symbolic, patriotic, and romantic.

Kate McClenny was born in 1868 on a farm near Lake City (FL) and lived in the Jacksonville area all her life. She taught piano and violin. The quilt was exhibited in Jacksonville's Roosevelt and George Washington hotels and was presented before the 1937 Florida legislature. It also appeared at Democratic Party meetings.

In 1945 the Jacksonville Beach mayor and city council adopted a resolution commending her for her vision and artistry. It seems fitting that this quilt so steeped in history and local pageantry now belongs to that city's Beaches Area Historical Society.

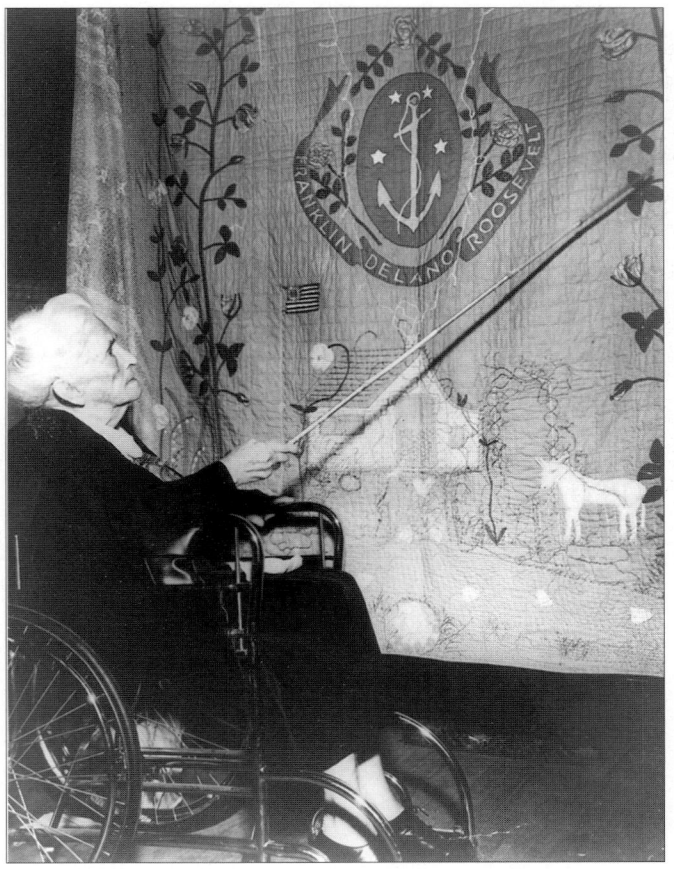

Catherine Elizabeth (Kate) Waldron McClenny, 82 years old, is shown pointing to a detail in her quilt. Photo: courtesy of the Beaches Area Historical Society.

Plate 3-39.
The Garden #4.
84" x 84".
1933.
Josephine Hunter Craig (1874–1954).
Made in Emporia, Kansas.
Cotton.
Collection: Dr. and Mrs. Paul R. Carpenter.
Photo: courtesy of the Kansas Quilt Project.
Documented by the Kansas Quilt Project.

During the second quarter of the twentieth century the quilters of the Emporia, Kansas, area were renowned for their skills and competitive successes. They went beyond the usual designs, adding elements and details not found in others' quilts. Their motivations seemed to be aesthetic and creative; they produced quilts for beauty, fashion, and as challenges to their needleworking skills.

The best known of the Emporia quiltmakers was Rose Kretsinger, a professional designer and co-author with Carrie Hall of *The Romance of the Patchwork Quilt*. She shared information with, and greatly influenced those around her. For years Emporians dominated state and local fairs and other contests. Most of these successful quiters can be linked directly through friendships or social interactions to Rose Kretsinger. An exception was Josephine Hunter Craig (1874–1954), a farm wife whose life did not appear to intersect that of Rose Kretsinger. According to research done by Kansas Quilt Project board member Barbara Brackman, "Craig seems to have had her own network of quilting friends with no personal link to Kretsinger, but the two national prize winners were surely aware of each other's work as they competed."[15]

"The Garden" won a first place ribbon at the 1936 Eastern States Exposition at Storrowton in Springfield, Massachusetts. The pattern was inspired by an antique quilt design considered the acme of the art of appliqué, seen in Ruth Finley's *Old Patchwork Quilts and the Women Who Made Them*. Records exist for thirteen appliqué quilts by Josephine Craig, "some of which appear to be original designs."[16]

Lois, Josephine, and Eleanor Craig.

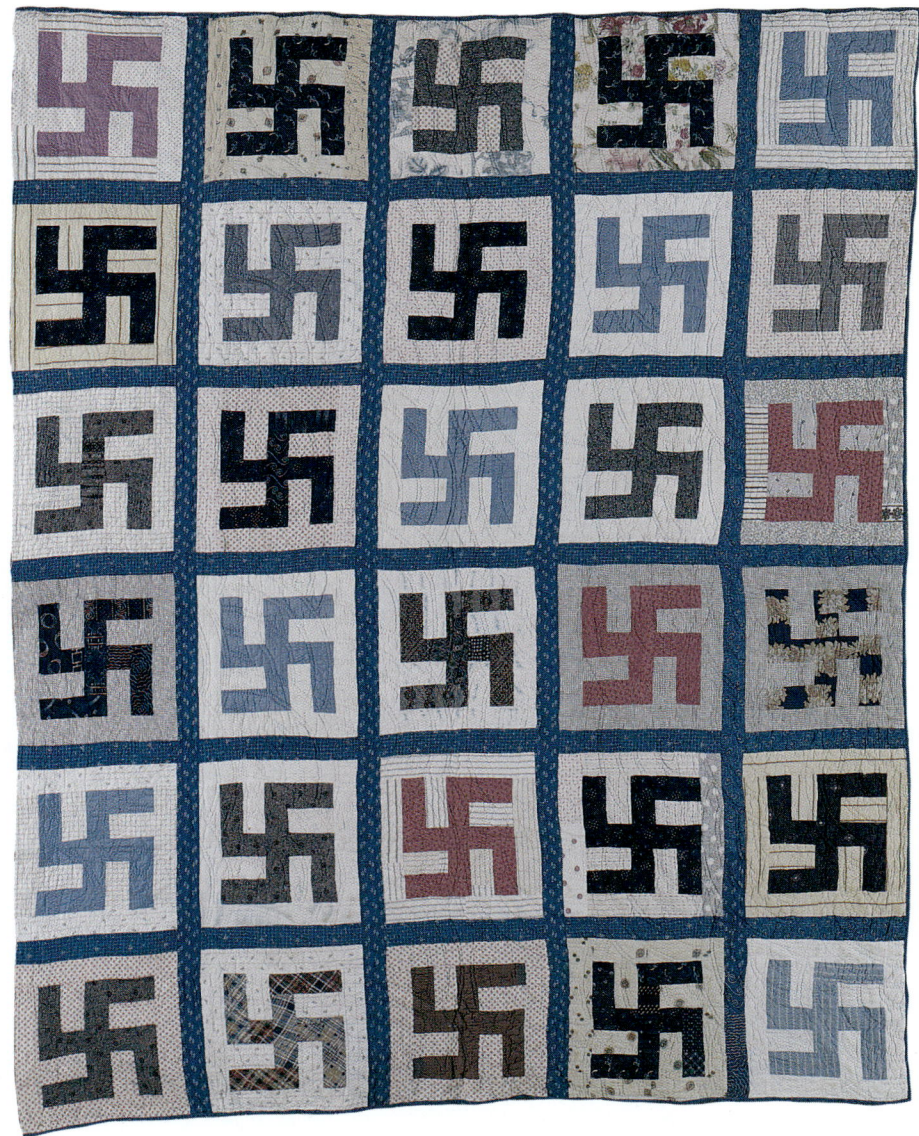

Plate 3-40.
Swastika Patch.
67" x 80".
c.1930.
Bertha Granfor Kier (1901–1987).
Made in Perley, Minnesota.
Cotton.
Collection: Connie Hulst.
Photo: Richard Walker.
Documented by the North Dakota Quilt Project (#18-6)

Bertha Kier wanted her great niece Mandy Hulst, now eleven years old, to eventually have her quilts.

The swastika or whirligig design has been around since prehistory and has been used in many cultures as a favorable symbol representing such things as infinity, the supreme deity, the four winds, well being, the sun's power, and the succession of generations. In the western hemisphere the swastika has appeared on pre-Columbian artifacts and Navajo baskets and blankets.[17]

Unfortunately, this ancient and distinctive graphic symbol now has the stigma of Nazism associated with it. After the rise of Nazi Germany the western world could only associate the swastika with evil. After the United States declared war, even the Navajo people were forced to renounce their whirligig design.

In a less public fashion many quiltmakers felt the need to eliminate the traditional Flyfoot or Whirligig pattern from their repertoire and keep from public display the quilts already made using it. According to the Arizona Quilt Project, Sarah Johnson Reas had made a Flyfoot quilt in 1910 and during World War II was told to destroy her quilt so her patriotism would not be suspect. Unable to do that, she hid the quilt away in an attic playroom.[18]

A similar story is shared by the North Dakota Quilt Project. Bertha Granfor Kier (1901–1987) of Perley, Minnesota, put her swastika quilt away at the start of the war and never used it again. The quilt was one of her utility ones, made from scraps and leftover material with a backing fashioned out of sections of flour sacking. The pattern had originally been chosen for its positive connotations, and bold and pleasing graphic quality.

So the pleasures of the Whirligig pattern, which had delighted Americans for so many generations, were nearly extinguished in our culture – prematurely, and perhaps permanently – because one nation chose to use it as a symbol of hatred.

Bertha and Elmer Kier. July 1940.

Plate 3-41.
Nine Patch.
126" x 111".
1840-1845.
Maker unknown.
Made in Moorestown, Burlington County, New Jersey.
Cotton
Collection: Historical Society of Moorestown.
Photo: Richard Walker.
Documented by the Heritage Quilt Project of New Jersey (#58).

Bible verses, family names (Stokes, Lippincott, and Warrington), and dates ranging from 1840–1845 are found in the center squares of this large Nine-Patch quilt bound with tan twill tape with a woven stripe, a type known locally as Trenton tape. Made in Moorestown, Burlington County, New Jersey, this quilt is inscribed to "Anna Warrington, Jr" even though it is known as the "Roberts Family Quilt." It was made by the Quaker friends of the prominent Roberts family of Moorestown.

This quilt has some of the characteristics of Quaker-made quilts documented by The Heritage Quilt Project of New Jersey – strips of printed material, blocks set on the diagonal, lack of borders, and a profusion of signatures or inscriptions. Along with these is a restrained color scheme. Quaker quilting designs were limited to straight lines or outline quilting patterns. Ironically, during the 1840s and 1850s when such fine Quaker quilts were being made, the religion was losing its hold on many members. According to project findings, Quaker quilt traits "are also typical of Southwestern New Jersey quilts in general, suggesting that non-Quaker quiltmakers in that part of New Jersey may have been influenced by Quaker style preferences."[19]

Plate 3-42.
Triple Irish Chain.
65" x 87".
1876.
Drusilla Showalter Cole (1847–1918).
Made in Moundridge, Kansas.
Cotton.
Collection: Jacinta M. Davis.
Photo: Richard Walker.
Documented by the Kansas Quilt Project (#DF51).

A Triple Irish Chain dated 1876 is the oldest proven Kansas-made quilt documented by the Kansas Quilt Project. The quiltmaker, Drusilla Showalter Cole (1847–1918), had come to Kansas from Illinois with her second husband, Thornton C. J. Cole, and her young daughter from her earlier marriage, Martha Bryant. They settled in Moundridge, McPherson County, in 1874 in a small cabin, but built a frame house as soon as materials could be shipped in. The original homeplace was added on to through the years and remained occupied by family until May 1992, at which point it was turned over to the city and became the Cole Museum.

The quilt was a wedding present from Drusilla to Thornton, made at the Cole homeplace. The Feathered Wreath and Star quilting was finished in 1876, a date Drusilla inscribed in the stitching, along with "from DC to TC," a heart, and a diamond. By this time daughter Mary Hasteltine Cole, the quilt owner's grandmother, had arrived. A son and three more daughters completed the family.

The challenges the family endured included grasshopper invasions. In a frantic effort to scare away the devouring insects, family members are said to have run up and down the rows of cabbages flapping quilts. Salvaged cabbages were chopped, made into sauerkraut, and distributed to hungry neighbors.[20]

This Irish Chain quilt, with its vine and leaf border, is tribute to the woman who juggled her precious time as wife, mother, and Kansas homesteader.

Drusilla Showalter Cole with her husband and children. L to R: Back row: Tina, James R., Nola, Mary (the current owner's grandmother). Front row: Zetta, Thornton Churchill James Cole (Drusilla's husband), Drusilla Showalter Cole, and Helen Bryant (daughter from a previous marriage).

Plate 3-43.
Kukui O Lono (Lamp of Lono).
87" x 77".
1921.
Meali`i Namahoe, Adele Kelley, and Maria Namahoe Kelley.
Made in Honolulu, Hawaii.
Cotton.
Collection: private.
Photo: Richard Walker.
Documented by the Hawaiian Quilt Research Project (#50).

Meali`i Namahoe Richardson Kalama (1909–1992). Photo: Lynn Martin, Folk Arts Program, Hawaii State Foundation on Culture and the Arts.

"One of the things I enjoyed about Mrs. Kalama was to watch her quilt. Her movement was so rhythmic, so unhurried, so relaxing. She looked so 'at peace' with herself it was almost mesmerizing. Her works reflect her spirituality and her God-given gift. She was so inspirational; we were very privileged to have known her and to have worked with her."

May Omura, longtime student of Mrs. Kalama.

Knowledge passes from one generation to another and the legacy of women of Hawaii is no exception. Kukui O Lono (Lamp of Lono) was the 1921 collaborative effort of a mother and two daughters. The quilt was to be a gift for their son and brother. The design inspiration is assumed to be the lamps at the entrance of Kukui O Lono Park on the island of Kauai and is believed to also honor the memory of Hawaii's Prince Jonah Kuhio Kalanianaole Piikoi. Thirteen-year-old Meali`i and her ten-year-old sister Adele were enlisted to help Maria Namahoe Kelley make this quilt. At the time they could not have realized that Meali`i Namahoe Richardson Kalama (1909–1992) would go on to be recognized in 1985 by the National Endowment for the Arts with a National Heritage Fellowship Award, and named a "Living Cultural Treasure."

A eulogy by her granddaughter, Lavonne Richardson Nakai, tells that Meali`i's *kupuna* (grandmother) provided lessons. The first lesson was to make a pattern for the *ulu*, or breadfruit tree, and that lesson emphasized the dual meaning of the word *ulu*. As a noun it refers to the tree which provides sustenance and as a verb it means "to grow." Lavonne explains, "Granny was taught that the work on her breadfruit pattern was important because through the work she would grow and thus gain wisdom and never hunger for it."

Lessons learned from her grandmother would be the basis for Meali`i Kalama's Hawaiian quilting classes. Elizabeth A. Akana, herself now an established teacher, historian, and designer, took lessons from Meali`i in 1969. She relates that sometimes participants would "bring the real thing to class like a breadfruit and leaves. We would take our inspiration from it and then the breadfruit was cooked to enjoy as a snack. Her classes were filled with fun and surprises...and always filled with love."

In an interview with Mrs. Lee Wild, Nana Aiu, who worked with Mrs. Kalama, commented, "When she was designing it just flowed out. I wish we had a videotape of her designing. Her designs were so graceful – there were no straight lines or angles." Interestingly enough, Elizabeth Akana relates that Meali`i felt the appliqué part of a Hawaiian quilt was "busy work" but the "only way to get to the quilting, which was spiritual."

To set the mood for the class, each session began with giving thanks. Elizabeth adds, "The love is still with us to see, to feel, to enjoy....She will live on forever in her quilts."[21] Those sentiments are perhaps echoed by many of the thousands who have enjoyed Meali`i's 30 Hawaiian quilts commissioned by Laurence S. Rockefeller to hang as art on the walls of Mauna Kea Beach Resort on the Big Island, or the quilt that adorns Queen Lili`uokalani's bed at Washington Place, the Governor's home in Honolulu.

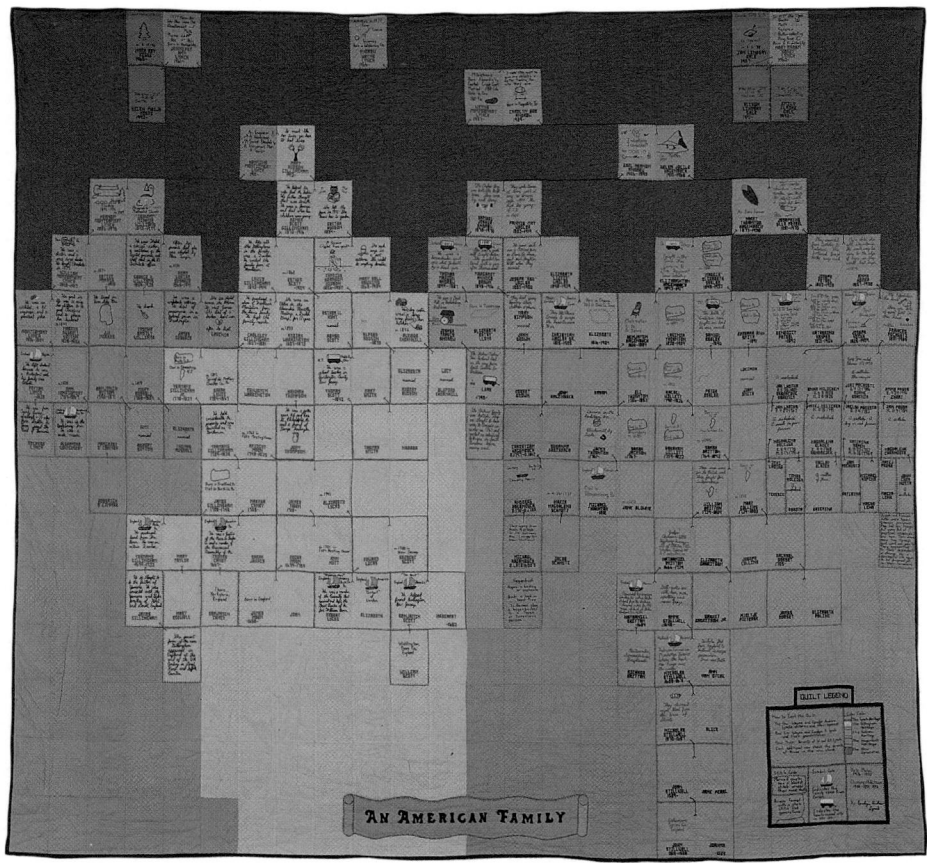

Plate 3-44.
An American Family.
96" x 88".
c.1978, additions in 1988, 1990, 1993.
Carolyn Lynch.
Made in Annandale, Virginia.
Cotton.
Collection: Carolyn Lynch.
Photo: Richard Walker.
Documented by The Virginia Search – Northern Virginia

Carolyn Lynch.

"An American Family" is an ongoing quilt effort by Carolyn Lynch of Annandale, Virginia. Her challenge "early in her quilting life" was to make a genealogy quilt. She confides that she was not deterred by the fact that she "didn't know what [she] was doing in either the world of genealogy or quilting." In its original form, the quilt took two years to complete. The three Lynch children took part in its making. Then, admits Carolyn, "It took on a life of its own."

Supplements to the 1978 original were added in 1988, 1990, and 1993, and updates will continue to be made as her children and their families branch out. Carolyn and Wayne Lynch's daughters have added Canadian and first generation Finnish-American husbands to their already interestingly mixed American family. Three young granddaughters make up the latest additions.

An exciting result of showing "An American Family" has been a new connection with others. In 1992 a friend's English sister observed that the oldest entry on the quilt was John Stillwell of Surrey County, England. Since Surrey was her home, she and her husband searched through records and actually found the old homeplace. The receipt of photographs of the house and lands was a thrilling moment for the Lynch family. Carolyn plans to continue adding information to the quilt.

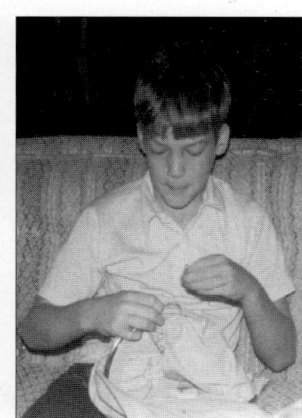

Everyone became involved in making this family quilt. Above: Carolyn, daughter Jennifer (age 16), son Andy (age 10), daughter Karey (age 14) at work on the quilt in 1977.

Plate 3-45.
Wool Comfort.
72" x 90".
c. 1880.
Anna Reed Smith (1848–1939).
Made in Oswego, Illinois.
Wool.
Collection: Clareta Walker.
Photo: Richard Walker.
Documented by the Illinois Quilt Research Project.

Anna Reed Smith with her granddaughters Clareta (left) and Lois (right), c. 1917.

Born in Somerville, New Jersey, in 1848, Anna Reed moved with her parents Isaac Farley and Ann Oliver Reed and two sisters to Oswego, Illinois, in 1854. In her younger days she was a school teacher and served as church organist and vocalist in the community. All her life she was practical and methodical, part of a family that believed in preparing for the future. Her wool comfort, referred to by her family as "The Old Wool One," is believed to have been made after the time of her marriage to Edward Austin Smith in December 1874. The couple raised a son and a daughter and the quilt became part of daughter Clara's dowry. The family has reason to believe that Anna's mother-in-law and Edward's two sisters, Susan and Louise, who lived on the farm just a quarter mile away, helped in the making.

This wool quilt of darkish colors was made up of many six-sided star blocks and is tied with dark red wool yarn. One of many quilts made by Anna Reed Smith, it was carefully preserved as a "best quilt" for company. On occasion it was used in severe cold weather in the unheated upstairs by her four granddaughters Winifred, Clareta, Lois, and Bessie (Bettye), who needed "a soapstone or two quarts of hot water and the wool comforter to keep warm." At that time household bedding was aired often, outdoors in both winter and summer. "Beds were never made up when you got out of them – [they were] always aired for at least an hour," according to Anna's granddaughter, Clareta Walker, the quilt's present owner.

An early twentieth century Smith family reunion.

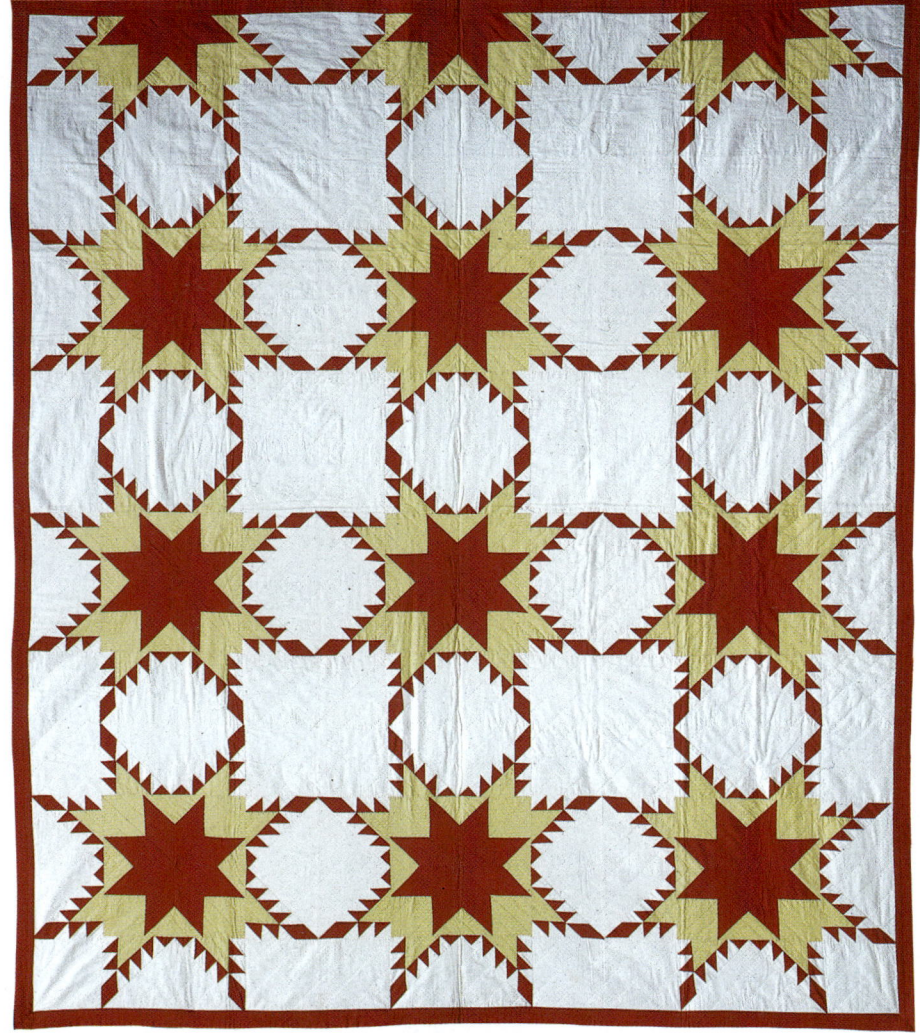

Plate 3-46.
Feathered Star Variation.
77" x 89".
1932.
Irene Fortier Betit (1905–1990).
Made in Middlesex, Vermont.
Cotton.
Collection: Hector T. Betit.
Photo: Ken Burris, Shelburne, Vermont, courtesy of the Vermont Quiltsearch.
Documented by the Vermont Quiltsearch.

Irene Betit, 1933.

"Her love was most often expressed in the work of her hands" and "Sewing became her craft and she honed it to an art form," were a few of the comments Cecile G. Betit chose to write in eulogy to her mother Irene Fortier Betit. Draped across the lower half of the casket at her September 26, 1990, funeral was the red and yellow on white Feathered Star quilt Irene had made in 1932. The floral arrangements had been chosen to match the quilt's colors. The altar cloth had been made by Irene's mother, Clarida Drouin Fortier, who had grown, processed, and woven the linen for it.

Irene Fortier was born in Saint Bernard, Quebec, Canada, in 1905, one of 14 children. She first came to Vermont at the age of 19. In 1934 she married Hector T. Betit in Bennington, and there raised their three children. Her daughter describes her as "a fine practitioner of the womanly arts." Irene Betit spun, wove, tatted, knitted, crocheted, and made fine garments, slipcovers, curtains, and drapes. She upholstered furniture, painted, gardened, and cooked. Moreover, she accomplished these tasks with enthusiasm! This quilt alone includes 1,560 individual pieces and the stitching of 11 spools of thread.

At the time of her death in 1990, Irene had looked forward to the next summer of 1991 and the opening of the Vermont Quiltsearch's "Plain and Fancy: Vermont's People and Their Quilts," a touring exhibition of quilts which commenced at the Vermont State House in Montpelier in celebration of Vermont's bicentennial. Her Feathered Star quilt was part of that exhibition and book of the same title. So important was this recognition that her obituary mentions both her skilled needlework and the Vermont Quiltsearch exhibit.

Irene and Hector Betit with their family:
L to R: daughter Madonna, daughter Cecile,
son Andre, and his wife Donna, 1989.

Irene and great-grandnephew, Guillaume LaRoche, 1988.

Plate 3-47
Crazy Quilt.
67" x 68".
1880–1890.
Jennie Quigley (1851–1935).
Made in Chicago, Illinois.
Silks.
Collection: Private.
Photo: Courtesy of the Louisiana Quilt Search.
Documented by the Louisiana Quilt Search.

Miss Jennie Quigley had a fascinating theatrical career that spanned 70 years. Her ambition was to visit every city she could, and she traveled to places like England and New Zealand many times. She performed for royalty, including England's Queen Victoria and King Edward, and other European heads of state.

Born in Glasgow, Scotland, in 1851, by the time she was four years old it was clear that she would be undersized. Her father, an artist who painted theater scenery, had been killed in a fall from a scaffold. Doctors advised Jennie's mother that perhaps help for her diminutive daughter could be found in America, so the family moved to Chicago. In school Jennie excelled and she could act, dance, and sing. With these talents she was soon supporting her entire family.

The 36" tall beauty made her debut in New York in 1864 singing the "Star Spangled Banner" for P.T. Barnum, who dubbed her the Scottish Queen. She performed with circuses, riverboats, and touring groups. From 1870–80 she was the prima donna of the All Midget Lilliputian Opera Company.

As she traveled she collected curios, including fabrics. She kept scissors in her pocket and would snip men's ties and keep the pieces. People gave her souvenirs and samples of fancy fabrics. Artists painted flowers on cloth for her. Since her mother made most of her clothing, she was able to add those scraps to her growing collection. In later years Jennie made this crazy quilt from accumulated cloth treasures. She sat on her tall chair and pieced and embroidered the four large blocks that make up this crazy quilt.

The present owner of the quilt, is Jennie's great-niece. Jennie spent her last days with this niece's parents. She told stories by the hour to their four children, who regret now that they did not listen more carefully to her exciting adventures.

Professionally, Jennie's final bow was at the age of 83 at the Chicago World Fair's Midget Village in 1933. She died in 1936. This crazy quilt is testimony to a unique person whose talents extended beyond the stage. The embroidered red silk handkerchief in the center of one block echoes, "In Fond Remembrance."

Jennie Quigley and her mother.

Plate 3-48.
Puff Quilt.
49" x 55".
Date unknown.
Maker unknown.
Silk, plain and brocade
Collection: Len De Angelis.
Photo: Courtsey of the University of Rhode Island.
Documented by the Rhode Island Quilt Documentation Project.

Visitors contemplate the 8,288 panels created for the NAMES Project AIDS Memorial Quilt, on display in Washington, DC in 1988.
Photo: Marcel Miranda III, courtesy of the NAMES Project.

School teacher Len DeAngelis serves as a Buddy in the Rhode Island AIDS program, which was set up to provide volunteer assistance for those battling this disease. "I try to keep them together before they die," he sadly comments.

This role introduced him to Bruce Natke (1952–1990), a young architect regarded as a visionary, who "designed space and created beauty with taste and quality." Bruce's love of nature was poignantly expressed during a trek through the autumn woods on a glorious afternoon when he turned to Len and asked, "Can you see why it's so hard to leave all this? How am I going to do it?" Shortly thereafter Bruce's health deteriorated and he moved to Florida to be near his family.

Almost six months later Bruce reappeared in Rhode Island, no longer needing his walking stick and miraculously sporting a 25-pound weight gain. In spite of this progress, Bruce realized he needed to consolidate his belongings. One Sunday Bruce gave to Len his much admired "Puff Quilt." It had been bought earlier at the Brimfield (MA) antique flea market; Bruce and his mother spied it at the same time, and they both fell in love with it.

Within a few months Bruce's biggest fear became a reality: he lost the sight in one eye. Len comments that for this person whose mission was combining visual elements, it "was an ax in the heart." When stays in the hospital became more frequent, Bruce's parents came north to care for him, and he died about a month later.

Because Bruce had valued his "Puff Quilt" so much, Len decided to have it documented by the Rhode Island Quilt Documentation Project. The volunteers noted this new twist on the role of quilts in this age of AIDS.

Their familiarity up until then had been with the NAMES Project AIDS Memorial Quilt, which represents an amazing spontaneous outpouring of amateur quiltmaking. Each of the three-foot by six-foot panels memorializes one of the hundreds of thousands of people who have died of AIDS. As of October 1, 1994, the quilt contained 27,730 panels, about 13% of the 220,871 reported United States deaths. It is a deeply emotional commemorative created by partners, friends, and families to bring attention to this epidemic, assist with HIV prevention education, and raise funds for community-based AIDS service organizations.

The silk fabric in Bruce Natke's "Puff Quilt" is now delicate and shattered, not unlike his life. But it is still beautiful, and Len has prepared a wall in his home where it will hang. This quilt given to him has inspired Len to make a Names Project panel for Bruce. It will be of puff squares spelling Bruce's name, "sewn on to a piece of very chic black fabric."

Plate 3-49.
Chintz Appliqué Medallion.
106" x 103".
c.1820.
Sarah Clark Willson (1782–1836).
Made in Clarksburg, Maryland.
Cotton.
Collection: Montgomery County Historical Society.
Photo: Richard & Ann Rohlfing, R.A.R.E. Photographic, Bowie, MD.
Documented by the Maryland Quilt Project (MO#196).

Sarah Clark Willson's "Chintz Appliqué Medallion" represents the efforts, determination, and dedication of the Maryland Quilt Project's volunteers to preserve and record as thoroughly as possible the state's quilt history. In addition to site days in each of Maryland's 24 counties and the city of Baltimore, the volunteers also documented quilts in historic societies and museums. One of those institutions was the Beall-Dawson House of the Montgomery County Historical Society, which has in its collection this chintz medallion quilt.

Sarah Clark was born in 1782, the daughter of John Clark, founder of Clarksburg (MD). From an affluent, landed family, Clark ran the general store and was the town's first postmaster. An 1806 estate inventory document which includes listings of fabrics and materials gives evidence that the store could have furnished all of Sarah's quiltmaking supplies from its stock. The store was run by Sarah's husband, William Willson, after her father's death.

This unusual circular medallion bedspread was made by Sarah in about 1820. The central chintz appliqué bouquet is surrounded by a carefully stuffed and quilted feathered swirl design. The crosshatched quilting stitches in this quilt shaped to be used on a large four poster bed can only be described as superlative. After Sarah's death in 1836, her quilted bedcover was never used, but was carefully passed down through succeeding generations.

The Beall-Dawson House, c. 1815 home of the Montgomery County Historical Society. Drawing by Carol Stuart Watson.

Plate 3-50.
Baltimore Bride's Quilt.
80" x 87".
c.1960.
Marie Fisher (1892-1971).
Made in Detroit, Michigan.
Cotton.
Collection: Lynne Charlet and Mary Lee Charlet.
Photo: Peter Glendinning.
Documented by the Michigan Quilt Project.

Marie Bradley Fisher (1892–1971).

Marie Bradley Fisher (1892–1971) spent the last 40 years of her life making quilts in addition to many other needlework projects. The mother of six, she was recovering from diphtheria and heart trouble in 1931 when she tuned to radio station WWJ in Detroit as it featured the *Detroit News* Quilt Club program.

Two years later she entered the *Detroit News* Quilt Exhibition. As the Grand Prize winner of that contest, her picture appeared in the newspaper. The photograph was recognized by her long-lost sister, Frances Janet Galton, who had been separated from her when placed for adoption as a result of a divorce more than 30 years earlier. At the time, Marie had been about four; each woman remembered having sisters, but they had not seen each other since.

Janet was also a quilter, and the reunited women became known as the "Quilt Club Sisters." Marie's contest-winning quilt "Horoscope" was given to Janet, and they enjoyed quilting together for many years.

The long years dedicated to the craft are obvious in Marie Fisher's "Baltimore Bride's Quilt," made about 1960. She continued to make quilts until her death in 1971. Lynne Charlet, Marie's great-granddaughter, and Lynne's mother Mary Lee Charlet are the current owners of Marie's "Baltimore Bride's Quilt."

Connie Wahrman, Marie's daughter, and Mary Lee Charlet, Marie's granddaughter.

Plate 3-51.
Signature Quilt.
67" x 79".
1901.
Mission Band, Cedar Street Baptist Church.
Made in Buffalo, New York.
Cotton.
Collection: The Buffalo and Erie County Historical Society (#80.119.1).
Photo: The Buffalo and Erie County Historical Society.
Documented by the New York Quilt Project.

Plate 3-52
Signature Quilt.
84" x 102".
1992.
Kenmore Quilters Patch of Kenmore, New York.
Made in Kenmore, New York.
Cotton.
Collection: The Buffalo and Erie County Historical Society.
Photo: The Buffalo and Erie County Historical Society
Documented by the New York Quilt Project.

On June 10, 1989, the Buffalo and Erie County Historical Society (BECHS) hosted a quilt documentation day for the New York Quilt Project during which over 200 quilts were registered. The New York Quilt Project day brought together two well-established organizations, the BECHS and the Kenmore Quilters Patch.

In conjunction with the 1990 exhibition "Patterns in Time: Quilts of Western New York," BECHS designed an activity to involve the community with the Historical Society. A "living history" quilt would be made to raise funds and become part of the permanent collection. The basis for the new quilt was a quilt already in the BECHS collection, a signature quilt made by the Mission Band Society of the Cedar Street Baptist Church in Buffalo, NY. Members of the Kenmore Quilters Patch offered to make the quilt.

The original sixteen block "Signature Quilt" consists of 240 signatures on white strips arranged like the spokes of a wheel on a turkey red background. Inscribed in the center is "To Mrs. G. Whitman from the Mission Band of the Cedar Street Baptist Church." It was presented to the Reverend George Whitman's wife when he resigned his post in 1901. The Mission Band, which is believed to have performed at prayer meetings, is also responsible for another quilt in the BECHS collection, one containing both images and signatures embroidered in turkey red on white. Both quilts are believed to have raised funds for missionary work.

The Kenmore Quilters Patch designed a 20 block quilt. The first four blocks were presold signature blocks for patrons, with one reserved for the makers. The first blocks were completed for the show's opening and used as sample incentives to sell signatures at the Museum. As each block was sold, the signed strips were delivered to the group for appliqué. By the end of 1991, the top was complete. Well before that date the group had worked out the quilting patterns which incorporated designs of architectural motifs found in the ceiling in the State Court of BECHS's Pan-American Exposition building. A special two day "quiltathon" was held, after which the quilt traveled between members for completion. The group estimates that 216 hours were spent in the hand quilting. In all, the quilt raised over $3,000 for programming and exhibits at the Historical Society. At the time the quilt was completed the Director of Museum Collections, Ms. Clyde Eller, commented: "These kinds of mutually beneficial relationships are an important result of the State Quilt Day projects."

Kenmore Quilters Patch of Kenmore, New York.

Plate 3-53.
White House Appliqué Quilt.
69" x 85".
1933.
Clara Louise Anderson Larsen (1870–1951).
Made in Roosevelt, Utah.
Cottons.
Collection: Reuben D. Larsen and Elizabeth L. Riedler.
Photo: Richard Walker.
Documented by the Utah Quilt Heritage Corporation (Provo #54).

Using a 5 x 7 photo of the White House, Reuben D. Larsen, an engineering student at the University of Utah, designed a quilt for his mother to make and enter into a contest. The winning quilt was to be a gift for Franklin Delano Roosevelt as he was inaugurated into his first term as President of the United States.

Then 63 years old, Swedish born Clara Louise Anderson Larsen (1870–1951) lived most of her life in Utah where she raised a very large family. She began quiltmaking as a child. For the 1933 contest quilt she used many remnants and sewing scraps including part of a parachute that she hand dyed for the windows of her White House. The work took three months.

Because Clara Larsen's White House quilt placed second, it did not leave the family. The contest judges confessed their preference for the creative design of this quilt but selected another which had finer stitches. Clara gave it to her son Reuben, the quilt's designer. He recently passed the quilt on to his daughter, Elizabeth L. Riedler.

Clara L. Larsen with her "White House Appliqué Quilt," c. 1935.

Fearful, in the way that Bruce Mann had been, of the growing anonymity of quiltmakers, project committees were overjoyed to find that frequently families had chosen to keep quilts and they often knew something about the lives of the quiltmakers.

Plate 4-1.
Pillow Cover.
22" x 22".
1906.
Mrs. Etta M. Cobban.
Made in South Dakota.
Silk ribbons, cotton, silk embroidery thread.
Collection: South Dakota State Historical Society (#1970.181).
Photo: Richard Walker.
Submitted by the South Dakota State Historical Society.

Campaign ribbons were political keepsakes generated for appearances by candidates at local rallies or events to "stump" for votes. Typically lithographs printed in black ink on white or cream colored silk, they were pinned on the lapel, and after the election served as bookmarks. They often had the names and pictures of candidates, pertinent slogans, and campaign issues, and names and dates of local events and their sponsors. The 1828 campaign of Andrew Jackson is thought to have been the first to use political ribbons. Relatively inexpensive to manufacture, they were generously distributed for most candidates from the 1860s until the 1904 election and are found in small numbers even today.[1]

Fortunes can be made or lost on the basis of where a capital or seat of government becomes located; and concern about the choosing of such a location was the theme of a commemorative pillow cover from South Dakota made of silk political ribbons. The chief battle in 1890 was between Huron and Pierre, over which would become the permanent capital city. Pierre, having been chosen temporary capital in 1889, was the victor. Near the geographic center of the state and on the east bank of the Missouri River, the city's name is derived from old Fort Pierre, which was the chief fur trading depot of the upper Missouri Country. In 1904, the city of Mitchell challenged Pierre to yet another capital campaign. The building of a permanent structure in 1910 finally settled the issue.

The gift of the pillow top was made to the South Dakota State Historical Society by Miss Franke Cobban of Worthington, Ohio. Her family lived in the Dakota territory where she, her brother, and a sister were born. Her mother collected the ribbons just before the Dakotas become states (1889), when cities were vying to become the capital. Included is also a ribbon for 1888 Republican candidate Benjamin Harrison and his running mate Levi P. Morton, who advocated "Protection for American Labor" and "Two States for Dakota." The various ribbons were collected and mounted on a muslin backing. The unfinished piece was to have been made into a sofa cushion. In 1965, nearing 80 years in age and with no heirs, it was Miss Franke Cobban's desire that the pillow top with its history stamped on silk ribbons be returned to its place of origin.

Plate 4-2.
Tumbling Blocks.
81" x 82".
1876.
Nellie L. Gates Ransbotham (1859–1927).
Made in Riverton, Connecticut.
Cotton.
Collection: Mrs. Edmund Holcomb.
Photo: Richard Walker.
Documented by the Connecticut Quilt Search (#717).

Nellie L. Gates (1859–1927).

Fourteen-year-old Michael Parker Ward left his Yorkshire home for America in 1823. Along with his brother James, he was in search of better opportunity. Poor and with limited education, the brothers would become examples of the American dream.

Befriended by the ship's captain and housed by him for a short time, penniless Michael visited the towns along the Hudson River in New York where he found employment in a calico printing mill. The boy's ambition and work ethic were noted and he was given a job in the dyeing department as helper to the color mixer. The dyer was not about to hand over his color knowledge to him, but young Michael Ward observed, memorized, and experimented at home until he mastered the techniques. After working in New York for several years, in 1831 he moved to North Adams, Massachusetts, and with his brother leased an unprofitable textile business and turned it into the profitable John Ward's Sons. When the lease terminated, the Ward Brothers and their father John, who had emigrated to the United States in 1830, moved to Hitchcocksville, now Riverton, Connecticut. There they built a new mill known as John Ward and Sons. The business prospered.

Michael Ward was a born entrepreneur and soon branched out into other business ventures including land, securities, lumber, and other manufacturing.

Nellie L. Gates (1859–1927) of Riverton was just seventeen when she pieced her "Tumbling Blocks" quilt, which included a great variety of fabric, some of which has been identified as being from the nearby John Ward and Sons mill. The backing was added later.

Nellie married George Ransbotham (1842–1895) in 1892, and they celebrated the birth of a son Kenneth the next year. Like so many children of the time, the little boy died before reaching his second birthday. George Ransbotham died just three months later. The husband of the quilt's present owner, Mrs. Edmund Holcomb, is a direct descendant of John and Michael Ward. Along with this quilt they have treasured another fine example of printed textiles, an 1836 swatch book of old fabrics from the same Wards' Riverton, Connecticut, mill.

Edmund & Dagmar Holcomb.

Plate 4-3.
Champion Ribbons Quilt.
88" x 90".
1959.
Mary Pardee for Mary and Purnell Friedel.
Made in Viola, Delaware.
Silk state fair ribbons and satin.
Collection: Delaware Agricultural Museum and Village (#92.30.1).
Photo: Kevin Heslin.
Submitted by the Delaware Agricultural Museum and Village.

The beautiful, flat, and fertile Delmarva Peninsula (DE) is renowned for its farms. The Friedel Farm, just outside of Viola, was known for its dairy cattle operation. Established in 1878, and honored as one of Delaware's Century Farms, the farm was taken over by Purnell F. Friedel and his wife Mary in 1927. Within a few years they began to show their cattle at the Delaware State Fair in Harrington, a tradition that involved their two children and continued for over thirty years. The state fair event was such an important part of their lives that, beginning in the early 1960s, Mr. Friedel became superintendent of the fair's dairy cattle department and served in this position for more than ten years.

In the beginning the Friedels did not do well in cattle competition. As is often the case with quilters and their contests, fair experiences compelled the Friedels to continually improve their herd of Holsteins. From "a few grade cows, we began to establish a registered herd," Mrs. Friedel recalled. Their efforts at improvement paid off, and through the years Friedel Dairy Farm won countless ribbons. They also showed their cattle in Richmond, Virginia; they rode the freight train, sleeping right in the cars with the cows.

Mrs. Friedel's task was to keep the records on each animal. "Our foundation cow was Carnation Josephine Betty, and most of our show cattle were her descendants," she remembered. "Betty" was nineteen when she died. In tribute to her Mary Friedel wrote a poem.

The next morning to pasture the herd slowly went;
Betty tried to follow, but her strength was far spent.
Nearly all were descendants, who passed her that day;
Going out to the meadows, sadly wending their way.
She was offered some help, to get to the barn;
But she preferred to stay, where it was sunny and warm.
When the noon day passed, old Betty was no more;
She had crossed the threshold, the last chapter was o'er.
In the front yard she rests, where she once loved to stay;
And crop the grass, on a long summer day.
If humans in their sphere, could have lives as well spent;
We could all pass on, with hearts full of content.

In 1959 Mrs. Friedel commissioned Mary Pardee, also of Viola, to make two quilts from some of her cattle's ribbons from the Delaware State Fair. After Mrs. Friedel's death one of the quilts made from Betty's ribbons was donated to the Delaware Agricultural Museum and Village in Dover (DE).[2] On the yellow satin background, a medallion of awards is arranged with the purple grand champion rosettes in the middle, surrounded by red ribbons and an outside circle of blue ones. A square border of purple champion ribbons completes the quilt. The Delaware Agricultural Museum and Village is a fitting repository for this quilt because the institution's mission is to bring the Delmarva Peninsula's rural past to life.

Plate 4-4.
W.P.A. Project Fan Quilt.
66" x 83".
1936.
W.P.A. Project.
Made in Davison County, South Dakota.
Cotton.
Collection: South Dakota State Historical Society (#1992.106).
Photo: Richard Walker.
Submitted by the South Dakota State Historical Society.

The Works Progress Administration, or WPA, was formed in 1935 as a Depression era New Deal program, the objective of which was employment on useful projects – work rather than handouts. While critics scoffed and referred to WPA as "We Provide Alms," during the WPA's eight years, nine million unemployed Americans were given jobs. While most WPA projects included large-scale construction – dams, bridges, hard surfaced roads, and public buildings, others involved service projects employing artists, actors, writers, and musicians. Two well-known examples were the Federal Writers Project and the Index of American Design.

One local project was the Museum Extension Quilt Project in Pennsylvania, which was responsible for the silk screened quilt patterns which have recently been studied and reproduced by the Variable Star Quilters of southeast Pennsylvania. This quilt group also produced *The Quiltie Ladies' Scrapbook*, and provided the nucleus for the Goschenhoppen, Pennsylvania, regional quilt study. Another WPA project which included the production of quilts was the Milwaukee (WI) Handicraft Project which has been documented by quilt researcher Merikay Waldvogel and published in the American Quilt Study Group's 1984 edition of *Uncoverings*.

In South Dakota, Davison County WPA workers presented Ethel Abild, the State Director of the Professional and Service Division, this 30-block Fan quilt, each block embroidered with the WPA project number and the name of a South Dakota county.

Plate 4-5.
Delectable Mountains.
74" x 82".
c.1929.
Anna Thoreson Starksen (1873–1953).
Made in Hetland, South Dakota.
Cotton.
Collection: Mary Ann Buck.
Photo: Richard Walker.
Documented by the Minnesota Quilt Project (MNQP#SJ037).

Anna Thoreson Starksen, born in Stavanger, Norway, was one of Minnesota's immigrant quiltmakers. She began her life in America in South Dakota, then moved to Minnesota, and ten years later returned to South Dakota. Newcomers to America seemed to adopt quiltmaking quite readily, participating with neighbors or with church groups. Anna was locally recognized for the quality of her work. When she quilted with a group, she was not above removing other's poor stitches and replacing them with those of her own high standard.

Anna led an involved life in small

town Hetland, South Dakota, where she and her husband Charles, owner of a general store, raised six children. She was responsible for most of the funeral preparations in the community in an age before there were separate commercial funeral parlors. She also acted as midwife as there was no local doctor.

In addition, Anna arranged wedding celebrations, and it is believed that this turquoise green and cream "Delectable Mountains" (or Sawtooth Diamond) was made in the 1920s for the wedding of her middle daughter, Geneva. The lovely hand quilting includes a feathered wreath in the center medallion. The edges are finished in prairie points. It is thought that her oldest daughter, Sadie Starksen Nielson, and possibly other Hetland women helped with the quilting. The quilt was eventually given, after being in the care of Geneva Starksen Larson, to the youngest child, Esther Starksen Buck, who until then had never received one of her mother's lovely quilts. It now belongs to Esther's daughter, Mary Ann Buck.

Anna Thoreson Starksen (right) with daughters (left to right): Sadie, Geneva, and Esther, c.1912.

Plate 4-6.
Tree of Paradise.
77" x 87".
1916.
Melissa Smith Deniston (1853–1922).
Made in Raymond, Nebraska.
Cotton.
Collection: Hazel Ryska.
Photo: Richard Walker.
Documented by the Boise Basin Quilters Guild Registration Project (#01159).

Hazel Ryska, 1992.

Christmas 1916 was a memorable one for the five Tally children. When they arrived in Raymond, Nebraska, to visit their grandparents, retired farmer Zephaniah and Melissa Smith Deniston, awaiting each of the children was a gift inside a well-tied, bulging white flour sack. At a signal from their grandma, three little brothers and two sisters, the children of her only child, Allie, "each made a dive and grabbed a bag from under the tree," recalls Hazel Ryska of Meridian, Idaho. "That" she says, "is how I became the owner of this quilt," a lovely blue and white tree pattern. Three other quilts in the Christmas bags included a Jacob's Ladder in peach and pale blue, a Maple Leaf in deep green with yellow and black dots on a white background, and a Bird in the Window.

Melissa Smith Deniston was born June 6, 1853, in Indiana. She quilted not only for herself but also for other people. In addition she served as neighborhood nurse and midwife and helped prepare the dead for burial. At the time she passed away in 1922 she had just started a Wedding Ring quilt. Hazel Ryska recalls, "Her stitches were still as fine as ever." "The Tree of Paradise" quilt has traveled from Nebraska to Kansas, on then Colorado and to Idaho, where it was documented. This graphic beauty now makes its home with Hazel Ryska's daughter back in Colorado.

Zephaniah & Melissa Smith Deniston, c. 1900.

Plate 4-7.
Appliqué Quilt.
86" x 86".
1877.
Emma Poovey (1850–1925).
Made in Lincolnton, Lincoln County, North Carolina.
Cotton.
Collection: David C. Heavner.
Photo: Richard Walker.
Documented by the North Carolina Quilt Project (#EB-57).

Leila Cline Baker (1872–1974), grandmother of the current owner, felt that this quilt purchased by her husband at an auction was too nice to use.

Probably no pattern found in North Carolina has stirred up as much interest as an unnamed appliqué which may have had its origins in a classic paper folding technique similar to that used by school children cutting paper snowflakes. The plume-like pattern seems related also to the fold-and-cut Hawaiian appliqué method. Most examples are found in the Piedmont area of the Carolinas, a section settled by both Scotch-Irish and German populations. About half of the examples can be attributed to the minority population of quiltmakers of German extraction. Recent study has found the same motif painted on the doors of a 1749 wardrobe made in Baden, Germany. It would seem that this pattern was brought by the German settlers and adapted to cloth. Some scholars have referred to it as a sun wheel. Some quilt examples are made of one solid color or blocks have six petals and all include reverse appliqué slits. The block centers vary and a few have added floral motifs, sashing, and/or appliquéd swag borders.

When David C. Heavner brought his appliqué quilt to be documented by the North Carolina Quilt Project, he had already engaged in sleuthing its origins. Not a family quilt, it had been bought at a Lincoln County auction in 1912 by his grandfather, E. C. Baker. The quilt, signed and dated by Emma Poovey, January 23, 1877, had been deemed "too nice to use" by his grandmother, Leila Cline Baker, who carefully placed it in a pillowcase and put it away in the linen closet. The quilt came into David Heavner's possession after her death. Delighted with and curious about the quilt and Emma Poovey, Mr. Heavner was able to contact the grandson of the auctioneer who had conducted the August 17, 1912, estate sale of D. S. (Daniel Sidney) Poovey, farmer and brick maker, Emma's bachelor brother with whom she had made her home. The auction records indicate that Emma's signed and dated quilt and other household linens were sold along with her late brother's farm implements and tools. It was one of ten quilts sold that day, and Mr. Baker purchased it for $2.25.

Emma Poovey was to live for another thirteen years until 1925. She made a will in 1921, making arrangements for "a decent burial" for herself and provisions for the graves of her father Emmanuel Poovey (1815–1892), mother Mary Summerow Poovey (1819–1887), sister Mary Jennie Poovey (1855–1904), and herself to be "fixed like my brother D. S. Poovey" at the Salem Lutheran and Reformed Church Cemetery in northern Lincoln County. She left bequests of two houses and lots, cash, her clothes, and a gold watch to individuals, probably cousins. She left bequests to Marvan Methodist Church and Salem Lutheran and Reformed Church. After her possessions were sold at public auction, the remains of her estate were to be divided between the Methodist Orphanage in Winston-Salem (NC) and the German Reformed Orphanage in Crescent (NC).

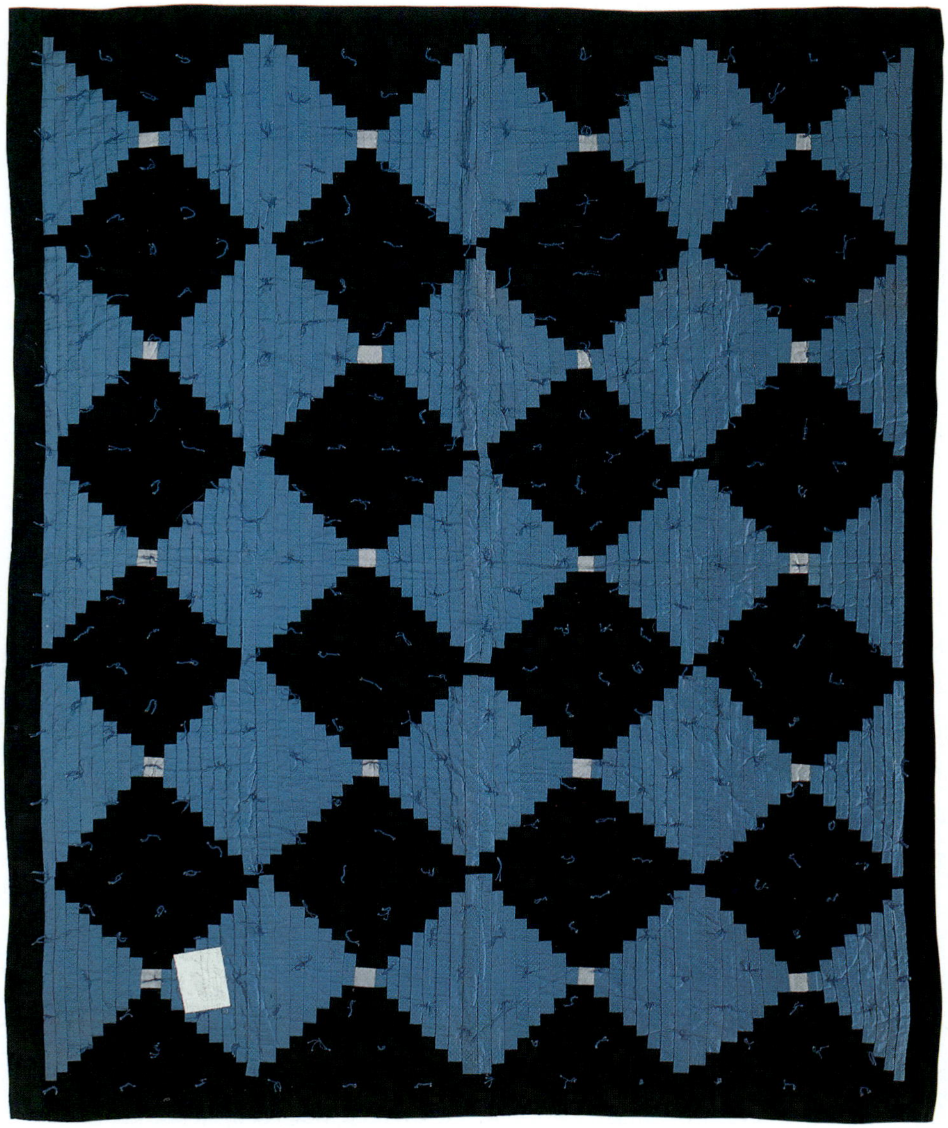

Plate 4-8.
Hap.
80" x 83".
1910-1914.
Cora Rute Keefer (1873–1950).
Made in Buffalo Township, Union County, Pennsylvania.
Cotton.
Collection: Gary and Donna Slear.
Photo: Terry Wild, courtesy of The Magazine ANTIQUES.
Documented by the Oral Traditions Project.

Cora Anna Rute Keefer (1873–1950) and her husband, Palmer Keefer.

According to Jeannette Lasansky of the Oral Traditions Project of Lewisburg, Pennsylvania, haps or rough comforters are not often the subjects of study because "they are not naturally brought forth by their owners, who consider them too dark, too heavy, too ordinary, and often too worn to be shown." Depending on the part of the country, haps are also known as comforts, suggans, britches, or hunting, camp, cabin, or fishing quilts and are usually made of scrap materials. The patches, which are wool or in some cases cotton, corduroy, or velvet, "are sewn on a foundation block-by-block and are assembled in either a random or patterned design." They are tied with wool yarn or heavy cotton thread and have thick wool or cotton batting.[3]

One such rough comfort or hap was rejected by a family member only to be happily adopted by another who valued family things, even if "dark and heavy." This pieced comforter was made in Buffalo Township, Union County, Pennsylvania, by Cora Rute Keefer (1873–1950) between 1910 and 1914. Gary W. Slear, who chose to keep the family textile, was rewarded for his careful custodianship when he removed a sewn cover and discovered underneath it a dynamic beauty in the Courthouse Steps pattern. A fabric tag sewn to the quilt reads, "Beulah/ was Grandma Keefer's, was on her spare bed. Never used."

Today haps are still being created. According to Jeannette Lasansky, the materials now include "trouser leg trimmings, denim castoffs, and double knits."[4]

Lula Edna Keefer Baker (1894–1971), daughter of Cora Anna Rute and Palmer Keefer.

Gary Wayne Slear, present owner of the quilt and his mother, Beulah Naomi Baker Slear, daughter of Lula Edna Keefer Baker.

Plate 4-9.
Basket Medallion.
65" x 68".
Pieced c.1890, quilted 1927.
Kjisti Erickson Peterson (1844–1925).
Inez Turner Baars (1896–1990).
Pieced in Towerville, Crawford County, Wisconsin.
Quilted in St. Joseph City, Arizona.
Cotton.
Collection: Ramona A. Bennett.
Photo: Richard Walker.
Documented by Quilt Heritage: Washington State (#3-593).

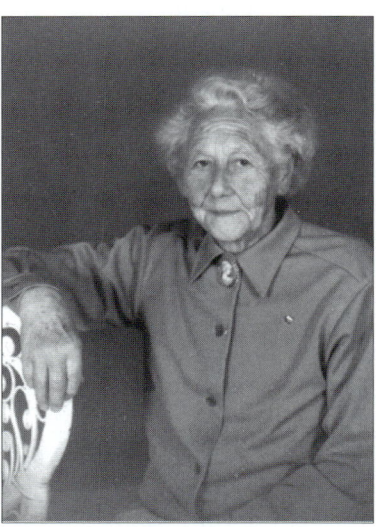

Inez Turner Baars, 1981.

This visually stunning blue and white basket design was Kjisti Erickson Peterson's last pieced quilt top. Kjisti and her twin brother Lasse were born in Hafslo, Norway, in 1844 to Eric Solvi and Anna Holsete Erickson. The young seamstress emigrated to Wisconsin with two brothers in 1862. Both brothers served in the Civil War, one dying during that conflict. After the war, Kjisti married Peter Peterson Midthum, also a veteran, and in 1874 they moved to a Crawford County (WI) farm, where they raised their family. One daughter, Christina (1871–1948) married Frederick Turner who lived on a neighboring farm. The Turner's five sons and one daughter, Inez, enjoyed a close and loving relationship with their grandparents next door. Inez described her grandmother as always being kind, loving, and cheerful. The "Basket Medallion" quilt top was a gift from her in 1913.

In later years Inez Turner Baars (1896–1990) learned to quilt. At the time she was living in St. Joseph City, Arizona, where quiltmaking was an important social function. The completion of her grandmother's "Basket Medallion" quilt in 1927 was just a beginning. The multi-generation quilt was brought to Washington State during World War II and now resides with Ramona Bennett, the quilter's daughter. She relates that her mother made over sixty quilts in her lifetime, 26 of which were documented by Quilt Heritage: Washington State. Also documented, along with Kjisti and Inez's quilt, were quilts by Kjisti's daughter, Christina Turner, and those by Inez's daughter Ramona Bennett, equaling four generations of quiltmakers. Ramona proudly reports that one of Kjisti's great-great-granddaughters is also a quiltmaker.

Kjisti Peterson and grandsons: Chester, Redford & Edwin Turner, 1905.

Ramona A. Bennett, 1994.

Plate 4-10.
Oklahoma History Quilt.
76" x 93".
1935.
Camille Nixdorf Phelan (1882-1946).
Made in Oklahoma City, Oklahoma.
Cotton.
Collection: Oklahoma State Museum of History (#4285).
Photo: Courtesy of the Oklahoma State Museum of History.
Documented by the Oklahoma Quilt Heritage Project.

Camille Nixdorf Phelan (1882–1946). Photo: courtesy of Archives & Manuscripts Division of the Oklahoma Historical Society (#6801).

Camille Nixdorf was born in 1882 in Missouri to Dr. Perry T. and Nancy Brumley Nixdorf. As her mother died at her birth, it was probably at St. Joseph Academy in St. Louis that she learned her love of art and needlework. In 1900 she married Dr. J. R. Phelan and moved to Oklahoma City the next year.

In the early 1930s Camille Nixdorf Phelan made her Oklahoma History Quilt because she felt that "in most of the published records...the sordid and rough element has been exploited to the exclusion of the cultural and artistic." She wanted to "depict the better element and to leave to posterity a record that will show the spirit of patriotism that motivated the great characters who made up the unique commonwealth Oklahoma."[5]

Camille Nixdorf Phelan made her quilt expressly to be donated to the Oklahoma Historical Society. As described by Carrie A. Hall and Rose G. Kretsinger in their book, *The Romance of the Patchwork Quilt in America*, "Using her needle she deftly embroidered each of the forty blocks that tell the story of the state's progress." Each block is extraordinarily detailed and includes prominent citizens, important events, and historic buildings. Hall and Kretsinger go on to describe the border as being "a clever arrangement of the flora and fauna of the state." They tell that the quilt took three years to make and that it was worthy enough to be shown at the 1933 Century of Progress exhibition in Chicago.[6]

Actually, the quilt's construction took longer than that. Two years were spent in researching and consulting. Camille felt frustrated at the lack of space on the quilt and was "forced to leave off many interesting incidents."[7] She carefully sketched the pictures she wanted to reproduce on to the cloth, outlined them in black silk thread, and embroidered the features. Twenty 100-yard spools of thread were used for the quilting. She claimed that this quilt took all of her spare time for four years.

The volunteers of the Oklahoma Quilt Heritage Project cheered Camille Phelan's motivation and realized that quilts *can* inspire and educate the public. This example brought the realization that one person's efforts should never be underestimated, and the impact of those efforts may affect generations to come.

Plate 4-11.
Carnation Flour Sack Quilt.
75" x 100".
1984.
Allene Loveless Pritchard.
Made in Lubbock, Texas.
Cotton flour sacks.
Collection: Allene Loveless Pritchard.
Photo: Richard Walker.

Allene Loveless Pritchard.

Baking for her extended farm family of 15 children assured that Sallie Eliza Bentley Beeland Loveless would have plenty of flour sacks available for making sewn items like dresses, undergarments, and curtains. When she married Samuel Allen Loveless they were both widowed, each with five children. Together they added another five. When financial times were difficult on her Lubbock County, Texas, farm, such as after a crop disaster, she would bake for the public as well. That situation made available even more flour bags! In the late 1930s she recycled squares from cornmeal sacks into a quilt, the decorative element being the printed portrait of Aunt Jemima.

When Sallie Loveless died in 1979 she left a set of 20 decorative Carnation Flour bag blocks, obviously saved for another quilt. One of her daughters, Allene Pritchard (1925–), was given the sack blocks to be made into a quilt. In spite of having grown up with quilting, Allene did not quilt. Faced with the challenge of continuing her mother's work, she learned to quilt in 1981. She outline embroidered all of the design elements on each of the 1925–30 era Carnation blocks, then set each one off with red fabric framing and sashes of green. She chose a simple crosshatch quilting design so as to not detract from the floral centers. On April 30, 1984, she proudly signed and dated the finished quilt, which she likes to display all the time, wanting everyone to enjoy it with her. Recently she discovered that the origin of the Carnation Flour bags was the Kell Mill and Elevator Company of Vernon, Texas.

Six Aunt Jemima quilts were discovered in the Grapeland, TX area by the documentation project conducted by the Texas Quilt Heritage Society. Two are pictured on page 107 of their book, *Texas Quilts, Texas Treasures*.

Sallie Eliza Bentley Beeland Loveless.

Plate 4-12.
Navy Yard Quilt Top.
70" x 86".
1847.
Ladies of Ebenezer Methodist Episcopal Church.
Made in Washington, DC.
White cotton muslin blocks, cotton appliquéd calico.
Collection: Mr. and Mrs. J. K. Cockrell, Jr.
Photo: Mark Gulezian, courtesy of the DAR Museum.
Documented by the "Made in DC" Quilt Search, Inc.

Signatures, dates, and locations inked on a quilt top tell only a small part of this quilt's fascinating tale. The rest of the story was supplied by the original owner's granddaughter and the careful sleuthing of the next owner's daughter.

The first clue in the tale is the fact that the "Navy Yard" top was never finished. Dated 1847, every block was made and signed by a different woman; each woman used different fabrics but ones that blended well with the other women's. There's no question that the quilt was made in Washington DC, for some blocks are inscribed as such or with "Navy Yard, D.C." or "Navy Yard Hill."

It appears that the makers of the top were a group of unmarried young women, members of a church serving the Navy Yard area, led by a 46-year-old-bachelor minister. According to information passed on to the current owner, Mrs. J. K. Cockrell, Jr., the minister's congregation decided to honor him with this evidence of their proficiency with the needle, and declare their esteem for their spiritual advisor. So they selected a pattern well known as "The Hero's Crown." The odd block is a pattern called "Laurel" – still a hero motif. Additional bible verses on some blocks, such as "We took sweet council together, Psalms LVc. XIVv," add to the drama. The top was presented to the minister before he left on vacation to his hometown in Pennsylvania. They planned to quilt it upon his return.

He returned on schedule, but with a bride, and the ladies saw no reason to bestir themselves further to complete the quilt. This was the information gleaned from the minister's granddaughter when she sold it to Mrs. Fulton (Elizabeth Saville) Lewis. Mrs. Lewis's daughter, Mrs. J.K. Cockrell, Sr., researched more. She found that the church was "Old Ebenezer" Methodist Episcopal Church located near Capitol Hill, the Arsenal and the Navy Yard on 4th Street near G Street, S.E. The congregation numbered about 400. Interestingly, the minister was transferred to a circuit north of Baltimore the very same year the quilt top was made.[8]

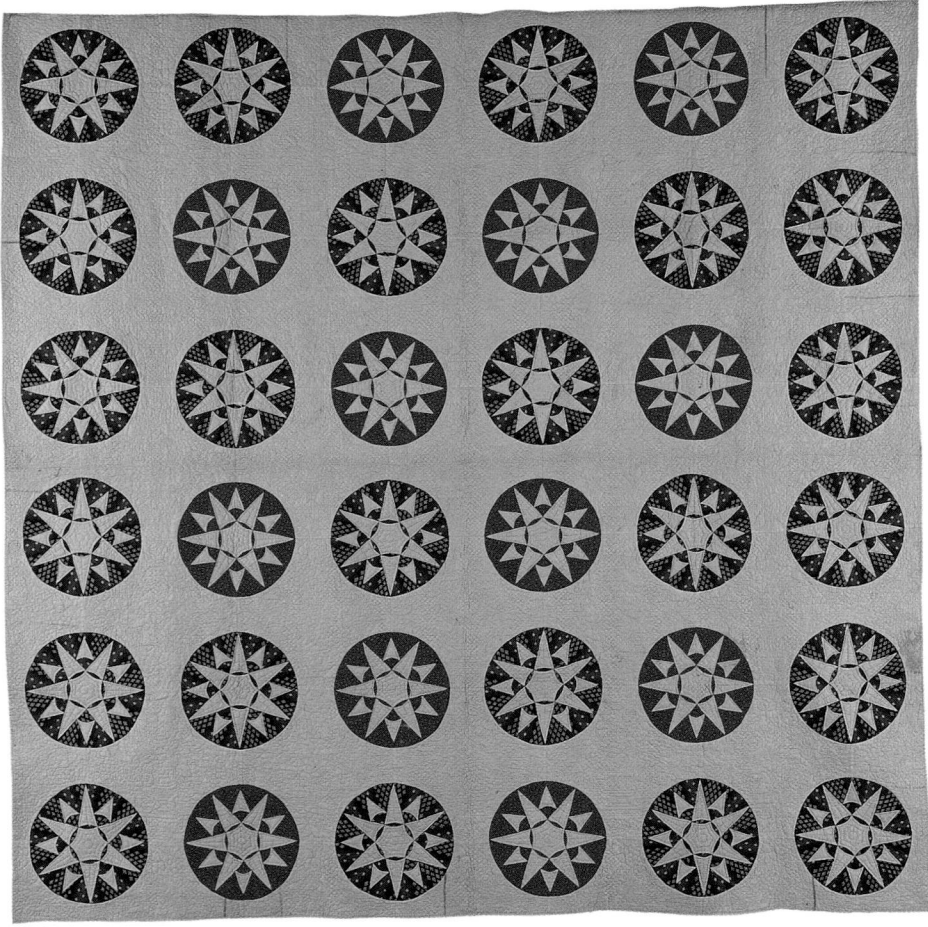

Plate 4-13.
Setting Sun Quilt.
99" x 100".
1841.
Annie M. Bender (–1855).
Made in Kent County, Delaware.
Cotton.
Collection: Mrs. Charles (Connie) Wahlig.
Photo: Richard Walker.
Documented by the Delaware Folklife
   Project's Quilt Day (#32).

From Kent County, Delaware, hails a large quilt of excellent workmanship, a Setting Sun pattern similar to a Mariner's Compass, made in 1841. The maker was Annie M. Bender (–1855), the daughter of Thomas Williams Wilson of Dover. The family was Quaker. When Annie finished quilting the lovely floral and grape motifs, she took the effort to both sign and date her quilt. No doubt she had the idea that this quilt would forever be regarded as "special." Over 150 years later, the quilt has remained unwashed and crisp, with the maker's pencil marked quilting lines still visible. Each generation has regarded it as an integral part of their family heritage.

Chapter 5

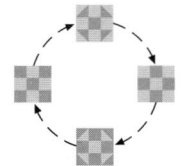

THE DISCOVERIES CONTINUE

Interactions and Results Greater Than the Sum of Their Parts

Although the files of many projects remain open for receipt of mailed-in forms, no documentation project whose exhibition and book have been produced is doing documentation; nonetheless, individuals are sometimes working on their own to write, often merely to add to or close the chapter on a particular quilt.

Between 1982, when the Kentucky Quilt Project opened its exhibition and issued *Kentucky Quilts, 1800–1900*, and the close of 1994, 23 states had completed projects. At that time an additional 18 had projects in process.

These projects sought to identify the quilts made or brought to their respective states. They hoped to learn what kinds of quilts had been made, where and when they had been constructed and, of great importance, who had made them. In some instances the progression within the family over the years could be charted.

As of 1994 roughly 157,000 quilts had been documented. In many states the data has been or is being computerized. In most instances, project files have been – or will be – turned over to state historical societies, appropriate museums, or university archives where they can be available for study. Only owner information has been restricted.

As Cuesta Benberry has noted: "The catalogs promise to be the major research work of the 1980s. They will, I predict, go down in quilt history as primary research efforts never before attempted. Whatever the selection process, whatever the approach of the project leaders, the central fact is, they are producing documents built on primary research. When all the projects are done, we are going to take a giant step forward in quilt history information. I am pleased that I am living while the body of work is being completed."[1]

Plate 5-1.
Broken Star.
118" x 118".
1835-1845.
Janet McCracken McCoy.
Made in Chillicothe, Ohio.
Cotton.
Collection: The Ross County Historical Society, Chillicothe, OH.
Photo: Vickers Photographic Studio.
Documented by the Ohio Quilt Research Project (#RCH2).

Like some other documentation projects, the Ohio Quilt Research Project had strict guidelines about using only quilts with a clear, verifiable provenance in their exhibit and publication *Quilts in Community: Ohio's Traditions.* In their book they featured a Lone Star quilt by Janet McCracken McCoy (c.1790–1841), reluctantly eliminating this more visually exciting "Broken Star" quilt from the same collection because they could not verify a maker or locale. A year after the book had been produced, new evidence was found revealing the maker of both quilts to be Janet McCracken McCoy.

As a child Janet McCracken moved to Ross County, Ohio, from Shippensburg, Pennsylvania. In 1808 she married Chillicothe merchant John McCoy, who had also come from Pennsylvania. Advertisements in the Chillicothe newspaper indicate that all the fabrics needed to make Janet McCoy's quilt would have been available from local dry goods establishments.[2]

Plate 5-2.
Blue Patchwork Cross.
76" x 80".
Pieced in 1895-1896. Quilted c.1930.
Pomona Louvicy Forester Stuart (1874–1937).
Quilted by Bertha May Stuart Boulton.
Made in Sugar Creek, Hickman County, Tennessee.
Cotton.
Collection: Martha Lou Boulton Shelton.
Photo: Richard Walker.
Documented by the Quilts of Tennessee Project (#1417).

Bertha May Stuart Boulton (1914–1992).

Pomona Louvicy Forester Stuart (1874–1937) had been married only a few years when in 1895 she began piecing her string utility quilt as a family bedcover. Like many other girls, she had learned the skill from her mother, Atlantic Turner Forester (1854–1938), who shared her patterns and fabric scraps. During the next year "Monie" and her husband Milton began building their Sugar Creek, Hickman County, Tennessee, house and she never got back to the quilt. Their daughter Bertha May Stuart Boulton (1914–1992) married Roe Jarrard Boulton in 1931 and lived in Cades, Gibson County. She completed her mother's quilt top then. The strong double set of sashing inspired co-chair of the Quilts of Tennessee Project, Bets Ramsey, to use this quilt on the cover of her book *Old and New Quilt Patterns in the Southern Tradition.*

Quilts of Tennessee chairpersons, Bets Ramsey and Merikay Waldvogel, are both examples of state documentation personnel who have continued to write and build on their research for further quilt study. Bets is more involved with contemporary quiltmaking, writing *Southern Quilts: A New View* with Gail Andrews Trechsel of the Alabama Quilt Search Project, and Merikay with Depression era quilts, having written *Soft Covers for Hard Times* and co-authored *Patchwork Souvenirs of the 1933 World's Fair* with Barbara Brackman, Kansas project board member.

Martha Lou Boulton Shelton of Tennessee proudly shares the quilt that was pieced by her grandmother and quilted by her mother. The five Boulton children had divided among them twenty family quilts prior to the 1983 fire which destroyed the family homeplace. Housed elsewhere, this quilt is one of the few remaining heirlooms. One sister, a quilter, convinced the rest of the family to have the remaining quilts documented by the Quilts of Tennessee Project, thereby preserving their history. This quilt was one of 30 Tennessee quilts in the state project's traveling exhibit and book. In accepting the invitation to show her quilt in the "GATHERINGS: America's Quilt Heritage" exhibit, Mrs. Shelton felt that participation would both "honor her ancestors' memory and preserve the American quilting heritage for her children."

Pomona Louvicy Forester Stuart (1874– 1937).

Plate 5-3.
Hydrangea Quilt
82" x 93".
c.1840–1870.
Maker unknown.
Location unknown.
Cotton, roller printed.
Collection: Lincoln Quilters Guild.
Photo: Nebraska Quilt Project.
Documented by the Nebraska Quilt Project (#4839).

Hydrangea Quilt, detail.
Photo: courtesy of the Nebraska Quilt Project.

The power of the national media in drawing attention to quilts is shown by the story of the roller-printed "Hydrangea Quilt" now in the collection of the Lincoln (NE) Quilters Guild. After an article appeared in *Collectors Magazine* about the Lincoln Quilters Guild Symposium of 1977, symposium chairperson Frances (Frankie) Best received a note from an elderly New York City woman, Fannie E. White, offering the guild a two-foot-by-two-foot section of an old "callicoe" quilt with an unusual print for a study sample. Anxious to preserve the quilt in its entirety, Frankie asked Ms. White if she would consider donating the entire quilt instead. Ms. White agreed.

The "Hydrangea Quilt" had been purchased by Ms. White in Poughkeepsie, New York. Ms. White, who celebrated her 103rd birthday in 1994, had learned to love antiques while growing up in Exeter, New Hampshire, where she graduated from the Robinson Female Seminary in 1908.

At first the owner's belief that the "Hydrangea Quilt" had been made around 1890 was accepted. However, knowledge of printed textiles, dyes, threads, quilt styles, and patterns has been expanded and widely disseminated in recent years. When the volunteers of the quilt project began their study of textile history that the quilt was carefully scrutinized.

Project member, Kari Ronning writes: "...when Frances Best organized the Nebraska Quilt Project in 1984, and its members began their training, the old quilt was recalled and brought to a workshop on textiles conducted by Dr. Patricia Crews (Department of Textiles and Design, University of Nebraska). Dr. Crews pointed out distinctive features that suggested the top might be an early example of the roller printing process. Project members learned to use the scholarship which was becoming increasingly available. They learned to look at quilts without preconceptions, and to work independently of an owner's suggestion as to the dates of old quilts....This old quilt, which the documentation project now dates to the period 1840–70, has taught so much to the quilt project members, who realize that learning about quilts must continue."[3] In preparation for this quilt's inclusion in "GATHERINGS: America's Quilt Heritage," a detailed analysis was prepared for the Lincoln Quilters Guild by Ann Reimer, ISFAA accredited appraiser, and Dr. Patricia Crews.

A distinctive feature of this quilt is the binding, made of what appears to be Trenton tape, as identified by the Heritage Quilt Project of New Jersey.

Plate 5-4.
Morning Glory Quilt.
60" x 86".
1887.
Sarah Berry (1819–1898).
Made in Hawkins County, Tennessee.
Muslin dyed by maker.
Collection: Mr. and Mrs. James Leonard.
Photo: Sharon Risedorph, courtesy of Mr. and Mrs. James Leonard.
Documented by the California Heritage Quilt Project.

Joshua and Sarah Berry.

A rather exceptional trans-continental connection has been made between the California and Tennessee documentation projects. "It was because of two state quilt projects that the distinctive Sarah Berry quilts were linked," writes Merikay Waldvogel of Quilts of Tennessee. "The state quilt projects have formed an important informal network by which quilt project personnel in various states can be located."[4]

Just who was Sarah Berry? Born in 1819, Sarah married in 1843 and settled with her husband Joshua in eastern Tennessee. Joshua served for a few months in the Union Army. It was in their home near Bull Gap in Hawkins County (TN) that their ten children were raised. Sarah made many quilts, including one for each of her 25 or so grandchildren. For the boys she made pieced quilts, for the girls, appliquéd ones.

When Sarah's "Morning Glory Quilt" was documented in California, the family's history linked it back to Tennessee. Project members were fascinated by the unusual style of the central medallion appliqué, the quilt's name of "Morning Glory," and the date "1887" with the maker's initials, a backwards "S" and a "B." They contacted Merikay Waldvogel to see if anything like it had turned up during the Tennessee documentation project. Tennessee project files revealed another quilt, this one dated 1894, with the same two initials.

James Leonard of California, the Berry's great-grandson, was able to provide genealogy and family addresses back in Tennessee. Merikay visited the community of Bull Gap and attended a service at the little church where Sarah and Joshua Berry were charter members. When the minister asked the descendants of the Berry family to rise, about 13 did so, and Merikay explained her interest in locating Sarah's quilts. Those descendants were able to direct her to others.

An exhibition of Sarah Berry quilts took place at the Fresno Art Museum (CA) from September 7–November 14, 1993, made possible by the support of the California Heritage Quilt Project. A small exhibit also took place in February 1994 in Rogersville, Tennessee, not far from the community of Bull Gap, where the quilts had been made. Both of these states and the quilt-loving public have benefited from the cooperative efforts of California and Tennessee documentation projects and the quilt owners involved.

According to Waldvogel, these quilts are important because they represent rural women who grew up "outside mainstream nineteenth century society without the benefits of schooling," where their recognition after "years of hard work tending farms, cooking meals, and raising children was sometimes only a few crudely carved letters on a churchyard tombstone." By signing and dating her quilts, Sarah assured herself of more.[5]

Plate 5-5.
Appliqué Quilt.
67" x 79".
c.1900.
Sarah Elizabeth (Betty) Friddle Smith (1862–1937).
Made in Eastern Guilford County, North Carolina.
Cotton.
Collection: Vickie Burleson.
Photo: Richard Walker.
Submitted by the North Carolina Quilt Project.

In 1971 Vickie Smith Burleson of Greensboro, North Carolina, embarked on her college career at Appalachian State University in Boone (NC). Her grandmother wanted to make sure she kept warm during the long mountain winters, so she sent one of the family quilts with her granddaughter. At the time, Vickie had little appreciation of a quilt's value, either as an heirloom or as a work of art. She relates, "It was just one of many quilts in my family – we used them for everyday purposes such as sitting or lying outside on the grass in summer." At some point Vickie brought it home and forgot about it.

Quiltmaker Amy Hecht Cook, Vickie's college roommate, was reading *North Carolina Quilts* shortly after it was published and mentioned to her mother, Rachel Baxter Hecht, a devoted documentation project volunteer, that she remembered a quilt like the one pictured on the back cover of the book. The quilt Amy remembered was the one from Vickie's college dorm bed. From her working with data in the North Carolina Quilt Project office, Rachel Hecht knew that this particular appliqué pattern was of special interest to researchers, having been found only in a small area of Eastern Guilford and Western Alamance counties. The large block with serrated leaves was rather unique. Amy visited Vickie with news about the significant pattern, and Rachel triumphantly brought the quilt to a documentation project work day where volunteers were coding computer data.

This, indeed, was the same pattern, and its maker, Sarah Elizabeth (Betty) Friddle Smith (1862–1937), Vickie's great-grandmother, had been a member of the same Evangelical and Reformed Church which some other makers of the quilt pattern had attended. She lived all her life in the area and was raised by her grandparents, Adam and Elizabeth Shepherd. Her mother, Delilah had died shortly after her birth, and her father, Private William Guilford Friddle perished as a prisoner of war in Elmira, New York, after having been captured at the Battle of Spotsylvania Court House in 1864. Betty married Thomas Arlendo Smith in 1883 and raised four children. A hard worker who did a great deal of sewing and gardening, her grandchildren remember her as being very stern.

Schoolteacher Vickie Burleson goes on to tell that just a few years ago her father, Thomas Vance Smith, gave her the quilt again, not realizing that his mother had already earmarked it for her. By the time of the second acquisition Vickie had gained a great appreciation for the art of quilting and had developed an interest in her ancestors. The quilt hangs on a bedroom wall where she and her husband see it the last thing at night and the first thing in the morning. She and Mike refer to great-grandmother Betty Smith as a "psychedelic granny" because of her choices of bold pattern and colors.

Each of the Alamance/Guilford quilts studied by the North Carolina Quilt Project is slightly different. While the quilt made by Betty Smith has only one border, most have three, with appliqué beyond the three-strip sash. Others simply have multiple strips. Sashing varies – three, five, or seven strips, all with corner squares. All quiltmakers chose vivid color combinations. One variant quilt has a tulip instead of a rose flower.

While many projects including North Carolina have completed the data-gathering stage, it is obvious from this example that the work of analyzing and selectively digging deeper into the documentation data from some particular geographic areas will be worthwhile.

Plate 5-6.
Scotch-Irish Quilt.
81" x 83".
1935.
Nona Thompson Rockwell (1903–1982).
Quilted by Mrs. Mary Linten Shipley and Nona Thompson Rockwell.
Made in Berkeley Springs, West Virginia.
Backing is muslin, filling is cotton, top is made of a variety of cotton fabrics including polished cotton.
Collection: Isabella R. Young.
Photo: Richard Walker.
Documented by the West Virginia Heritage Quilt Search, Inc.

Isabella Young remembers well her mother's friend who came to help quilt because that neighbor "was a double for the Dutchess of Windsor." Mary Linten Shipley (Mrs. Joe) was a registered nurse who lived close to her good friend, Nona Thompson Rockwell and liked to learn to sew and quilt with her. In 1935 the two friends quilted a top that Nona Rockwell (1903–1982) had pieced. A housewife and seamstress, Nona and her teacher/carpenter husband raised two daughters in Berkeley Springs, Morgan County, West Virginia. Although an accomplished needleworker, Mrs. Rockwell did not piece quilts until after her marriage in 1922.

During the Depression years she took in sewing and made all of her daughters' clothes. Her lifelong skills and interest in art and drawing later led to teaching oil painting and ceramics for many years.

Fawn Valentine of the West Virginia Heritage Quilt Search noticed a characteristic about this quilt that she feels has appeared in many of the West Virginia scrap quilts done by women of Scotch-Irish descent. Although the Scotch-Irish were some of the earliest settlers in West Virginia, they thought of themselves as different from the mainstream population, living apart from Germans and English. The Scotch-Irish look "is characterized by the use of two different printed fabrics – often having the same value – in a pieced block. The effect can be that of the color blindness tests: can you find the pattern hidden in the swirling colors?" Fawn also feels that the use of two or more adjacent printed fabrics in a pieced block is still practiced today by makers with Scotch-Irish heritage, and as far as she can tell is a practice acquired through contact with family quilts. She continues to study this theory.

Nona T. Rockwell (1903–1982).

Mary E. Bealle, daughter of the maker. Mary had the quilt in her possession but never used it. She gave it to her sister, Isabella, the current owner in 1991.

Isabella R. Young, daughter of maker and current owner of the quilt.

Plate 5-7.
Child's Quilt.
33" x 60".
After 1836.
Martha Jane Singleton Hatter Bullock (1815–1896).
Made in Greensboro, Alabama.
Crocheted edging and fringe, chintz, white embroidery.
Collection: Helen and Robert Cargo.
Photo: Birmingham Museum of Art.
Documented by the Alabama Quilt Search.

The theme of women rising to the occasion is not a new one. Women whose men go to war can be the most passioned and certainly every Southern household was affected by the Civil War in some manner. Women's patriotism was called upon in both the North and South to help outfit, clothe, and provide bedding and bandages for their soldiers.

The call went out for another Confederate cause in late 1861. Funds needed to be raised for the defense of the Confederacy, particularly to build gunboats to defend port cities. The Women's Gunboat Fund was an idea that was spawned in New Orleans but spread rapidly to Alabama and other parts of the South including South Carolina, Georgia, and Virginia. In an intense plea on February 18, 1862, the Mobile newspaper reported that "if the women take it up with a will, there is no such word as fail."

One such woman who took the words to heart was Martha Jane Singleton Hatter Bullock (1815–1896) of Greensboro, Alabama. A widow with two sons in uniform, Martha Jane Hatter was involved in the fund-raising, which included concerts, raffles, bazaars, and dinner parties. At least six quilts were donated to the Alabama cause and two of those have been attributed to Mrs. Hatter. They are now in the collections of the Birmingham Museum of Art and the First White House of the Confederacy in Montgomery, where a child's quilt of hers is also in the collection. All three quilts are of medallion style and are showcase quality rather than functional bed quilts. Each exhibits superior needlework skill and includes cutout appliqué, fine embroidery, and stuffed work.

We do know that each of the Martha Jane Hatter gunboat quilts was auctioned and donated back to be auctioned again for more funds, one of them eventually being sold four times. The Women's Gunboat Fund flourished for a short time until public enthusiasm fell after a series of Confederate defeats resulted in the destruction of most of the ironclads. Gunboat funds were then redirected to medical purposes.

Another child's quilt was purchased in 1989 from the estate of a descendant of Colonel William Henley Bullock, whom Martha Jane Hatter had married in 1863. This crib quilt appears clearly related to the other three Martha Jane Hatter quilts in both style and skill of workmanship. This piece, like the other child's quilt, has fringes, applied floral chintz fabric on a plain ground, and is overall quilted.[6]

The works of this Alabama patriot have been meticulously studied by Bryding Adams, Curator of Decorative Arts at the Birmingham Museum of Art and by the Alabama Quilt Search. Robert and Helen Cargo, owners of this crib quilt, have put it on extended loan to that facility. Scholars and quilt lovers, they hope that other quilts like this example or other gunboat quilts will surface. Because Martha Jane Singleton had her beginnings in New Bern, North Carolina, and Richard B. Hatter in South Carolina, perhaps that thread will extend beyond state boundaries.

Plate 5-8.
Relampago (Lightning).
53" x 74".
1945.
Elena Aguilar Sanchez (1911–).
Made in Questa, New Mexico.
Cottons.
Collection: Priscilla Gaillour.
Photo: Richard Walker.
Documented by the Survey of the Hispanic Quiltmaking Tradition in Taos County.

When folklorist Jeannette Lasansky came to New Mexico a decade ago to do a quilt survey she probably had little idea of the enthusiasm she would kindle in a local quilter, Dorothy Zopf, to discover and record the quiltmaking heritage in the mountain villages of northern Spanish New Mexico.

A strong tradition of patchwork continues to flourish there as a practical activity to create objects of warmth and utility as well as decoration. "Now we make quilts because we're addicted. Keeps us out of mischief..." chuckles one area quiltmaker.[7]

Today the quilts contain every conceivable type of fabric, but the construction technique, tying, harkens back to the days of wool, when quilts needed to be disassembled for cleaning. The fillers are now sheet blankets or older quilts. The frugality of these quilts and the often startling juxtaposition of colors and fabrics is a direct result of the need for self-sufficiency in a fading and marginal farming economy.

Here a majority of the population descends from the area's early Spanish colonists. Elena Aguilar Sanchez was born in 1911 in Questa, New Mexico Territory, and still lives in a small adobe house in the family compound. Spanish is her only language. She has always made quilts for pin money and depends on family near and far to keep her supplied with materials.

"Relampago" or "Lightning" was made about 1945, for a neighbor. Quilt size was determined by bed size, because Elena stores her quilts between the mattress and bed springs in her small home.

Elena Aguilar Sanchez.

Plate 5-9.
Nine-Patch on Point.
80" x 83".
Pieced 1909-1910, quilted 1920.
Kathryn H. Bomberger,
  her sister, and their mother.
Made in Lititz, Pennsylvania.
Cottons.
Collection: Kathryn H. Bomberger.
Photo: Richard Walker.
Documented by Lancaster County Quilt
  Harvest.

Lancaster County Quilt Search volunteer Jane Bibleheimer of Lititz, Pennsylvania, has developed an ongoing relationship with one of the individuals who brought quilts to be documented. A regular quilt day volunteer, Jane was assigned to register the quilts of 90-year-old Kathryn Hostetter Bomberger. During the interview, Jane asked about related pieced or quilted items at home. The scope of this documentation project includes petticoats, tops, templates, pieced bags, pillowcases, pincushions, and the like. Kathryn invited the project personnel to come to her home. Jane visited and recalls: "I was asked to follow her to her bedroom. She opened a wonderful old chest at the foot of her bed and carefully lifted out her childhood doll. Kathryn took out several more quilts and a great pillowcase cover (pieced work) which she said was hung in the outhouse to hold sheets of paper." Those items were also documented by the project.

The women's friendship grew and Jane loved hearing Kathryn's stories of growing up on a Lancaster County farm. At 90, Kathryn continues to plant, harvest, and prepare food for freezing. According to Jane, it is when she is involved in such activities that she is happiest. She loves sharing her fresh vegetables with friends. She knits scarves and slippers for a church mission project and stays informed about the world. If having difficulty with a task, Kathryn's attitude is, "If you can't go in the front door, you just go around back!" Quilt project friends Jane and Kathryn, "try to visit once or twice a month for a lunch outing."

This Nine-Patch quilt was made by Kathryn, her sister, and their mother. The piecing was done in 1909–1910 and the quilting ten years later. Kathryn admitted that she didn't like the hand piecing because she couldn't do it as well as her sister and mother could, but she felt she could quilt better than they.

Kathryn Hostetter Bomberger and Jane Bibleheimer, 1995.

Plate 5-10.
Lone Star with Broderie Perse #12.
84" x 85".
c.1850.
Maker unknown.
Descended in the Clegg family, New Jersey.
Cottons.
Collection: Hilary Elizabeth Reuben (age 13) a Clegg descendent.
Photo: The Heritage Quilt Project of New Jersey.
Documented by The Heritage Quilt Project of New Jersey.

This "Lone Star with Broderie Perse Quilt" was part of the family inheritance of the Clegg family of West Orange, New Jersey. The family owned a florist business there, not far from the Victorian mansion and laboratory of Thomas Edison. While the family is not sure of the quilt's specific origins, its previous owner, Caroline Clegg (1875–1950), was known for her exquisite taste. She treasured "The Quilt," as it was referred to by family, and kept it in a trunk in the front hall. Believed to have been made about 1850, the center of the star is made of a single circle of blue fabric with a gold sunburst appliquéd to it. Gold chain stitching represents the sun's rays, and the image seems to pulsate. Chintz appliqués are beautifully worked in a buttonhole stitch of red thread. The corner motifs are ringed in laurel leaves.[8]

Because the Heritage Project of New Jersey chose to include a chapter in their book on the quilts of one family (Clegg/Dunlap) which included the Lone Star quilt belonging to young Hilary Reuben, the family's knowledge of its branches have been extended. According to Hilary's mother, Gail Dunlap Reuben, who contributed research on the family tree, new relatives have been discovered and contact with out-of-touch branches has been re-established.

Probably the children have benefited the most. In a letter to the project, Gail wrote: "I do want to thank you....Each night on our family's summer vacation we worked on our family tree. My parents told stories of their childhood and shared other memories that very likely would have been lost with their generation." When Hilary was to be photographed for a newspaper story with her quilt, she sought out and wore the cameo pin that her great-grandmother, Lizzie Hiler Dunlap, wears in the photograph that appeared in *New Jersey Quilts – 1777 to 1950*.

Hilary Elizabeth Reuben and her grandmother Edna Dunlap with Hilary's Lone Star quilt.
Photo: Bergen Record.

Plate 5-11.
Milwaukee's Own (Mississippi Oak Leaf).
83" x 68".
c.1880.
Minerva C. Shell (1842–1913).
Made in Knox County, Tennessee.
Cotton.
Collection: Kitty Cornett.
Photo: Richard Walker.
Documented by Quilts of Tennessee.

When Kitty Cornett brought her great-great-grandmother's quilt to be documented as part of the Quilts of Tennessee project in 1985, she had no idea that this would eventually lead to her meeting another quilt owner who was related. Looking back through the records of the Knoxville quilt day, volunteers noticed that an unusual background quilting design which had been documented resembled one they had found earlier in the day. After comparing the records they realized that the makers of the quilts were first cousins. The related quilt owners were contacted and put in touch with each other. They showed their quilts and liked to imagine that perhaps the two cousins had helped and advised one another when making each quilt.

The 30 pieced blocks in Minerva C. Shell's quilt are a pattern known as Milwaukee's Own or Mississippi Oak Leaves and the blocks are quilted individually with a background of concentric squares. The plain blocks are quilted with a distinctive sunflower design.

A quiltmaker's individualistic style and alert volunteers were responsible for this reunion. Other projects have "small world" stories about connections brought about by quilts. In Utah, when volunteers were documenting quilts in a museum collection, a helper was amazed to discover that her great-grandmother had created one of them. Equally exciting is a tale from Iowa, where a documentation day was interrupted by commotion when a volunteer interviewer recording a history realized that she was related to the quilt owner. Both parties were thrilled by the discovery.

In September of 1990, an extension agent from Wicomico County on the eastern shore of Maryland organized a bus trip to the Maryland Quilt Project Show held in Timonium. At the show, one of the group was reading a signature quilt and turned to mention to his companions that he was related to a person whose name appeared on the quilt. A voice from behind him echoed that she, too, was related to the very same person. Prior to that event, neither had been aware of their relationship.

Viva Mynatt Majors, daughter of Minerva C. Shell, and her second husband, Columbus.

Madge Mynatt Lewis, daughter of Viva Mynatt Majors and her own daughter, Jane.

Jane Perdue Lewis Cornett, daughter of Madge Mynatt Lewis.

Katherine (Kitty) Patricia Cornett, daughter of Jane Perdue Lewis Cornett, and current owner of quilt.

Plate 5-12.
Pomegranate Quilt.
98" x 108".
1859.
Mary Elizabeth Lynes White (1834–1866).
Made in Missouri.
Collection: Alice Lee Harris.
Photo: Sharon Risedorph.
Documented by the California Heritage Quilt Project.
Photos: courtesy of Alice Lee Harris.

Logo of clasped hands on gravestone of Mary Elizabeth Lynes, wife of James H. White, Bonne Femme Church, Columbia, Missouri.

Quiltmaking as an art was shared by two sisters, Mary Elizabeth Lynes and Laura Lynes. Mary's quilt was documented in California, Laura's in Missouri. When Jean Ray Laury, author of *Ho for California* (the California project book), noted the Mary Elizabeth Lynes quilt had been made in Missouri, she called Bettina Havig, author of *Missouri Heritage Quilts*. Hearing a description of the quilt, Bettina referred Jean to the Laura Lynes quilt in the Missouri book. Eventually the California owner of the Mary Lynes quilt was put in touch with relatives who owned the Laura Lynes quilt in Missouri.

Mary Elizabeth Lynes White's tombstone in the Bonne Femme Church graveyard is carved with an image of clasped hands. She died in 1866 in Columbia, Missouri, just five years after her marriage to James Harrison White. James, son of a Methodist minister, was a farmer and merchant. She left three little children — Alice Lee, Emma, and Claude.

The clasped hand image resembles one she had carefully stitched into her engagement quilt, a Pomegranate appliqué dated 1859. This was made while she waited for James to return from duty in the Union Army. Additional motifs included an American eagle, hearts entwined, and the mottoes *e pluribus unum* (one out of many) and *salus populi suprema* (the supreme horn is the salvation of the people).

This quilt is a testimony of the feelings of the quilter at this critical time in American history, and also she and her husband's love for each other. In the 1900s the quilt was shown in county fairs, winning ribbons and silver spoons.

James Madison Lynes, father of Mary Elizabeth and Laura Lynes.

Hannah B. (Victor) Lynes, mother of Mary Elizabeth and Laura Lynes.

Alice Lee Harris, great-granddaughter and Barbara Holmberg, great-great-granddaughter of Mary Elizabeth Lynes.

Plate 5-13.
Love Apple and Rose.
68" x 83".
c.1889.
Laura E. Lynes (1854–1921).
Made in Boone County, Missouri.
Cotton.
Collection: Mrs. James M. Peeler.
Photo: Courtesy of the American Quilter's Society.
Documented by the Missouri Heritage Quilt Project (#19).

Mary and Laura were the daughters of James Madison and Hannah B. Victor Lynes. Mary was the eldest of 11 children born between 1834 and 1860. James and Hannah Lynes made their home with their second-born daughter Sarah and her husband John Beazley. The household included Laura E. Lynes, the sister 20 years Mary's junior.

In 1889 when she was 35 years old, Laura, who did not marry, completed "Love Apple and Rose." She included in her quilt many similar features to those found in Mary's, including the same pomegranate appliqué, same quilted clasped hands, and a similar appliquéd border, although Laura chose to apply hers with a fine treadle machine straight stitch. The family has noted that the same templates were used in Laura's quilt. This quilt was documented as part of the Missouri Heritage Quilt Project.

Because the Laura Lynes quilt had been published, the owner of the Mary Lynes quilt, Alice Lee Harris of California was able to make contact with her cousin, the late James Peeler, in Missouri. Mr. Peeler was the grandson of Minnie, the youngest daughter of James and Hannah Lynes. Alice Lee Harris is the great-granddaughter of the eldest, Mary. After a trip to Missouri in search of her roots, Alice Lee Harris writes, "One thing I have learned from this research is the importance of one quilt and how it contributed to the legacy of a family." James Peeler was interested in family history and was able to share photographs and records with the California cousin he had never met before.

Laura Elizabeth Lynes.

Plate 5-14.
Marine Mammal Quilt.
74" x 91".
1988.
Melody Stolzfus Chesley with
*   Pratt Museum Volunteers.*
Made in Homer, Alaska.
Collection: Pratt Museum.
Photo: Richard Walker.
Submitted by the Pratt Museum.

While the state of Alaska has yet to begin a formal documentation project, the community of Homer has had a unique endeavor of its own going on since 1981. The small town of Homer is known for its arts, its fishing, and its support of the environment. One of their proudest achievements is the Pratt Museum / Homer Society of Natural History.

For nine months each year quilters gather at this museum to design and sew two natural history theme quilts — one to raffle to raise funds, the other for the Museum's permanent collection. According to Elizabeth A. (Betsy) Webb, Curator of Collections, "Experience has shown that building a permanent collection of natural history theme quilts draws on the artistic strength of local quilters, maintains a community tradition, reinforces the Museum as a focal point of community energy and cooperation, contributes to the programmatic diversity of Museum exhibits, raises significant funds for the Museum's operations, and is downright fun."

Melody Stoltzfus Chesley was involved in the 1988 quilts. Though she was a beginning quilter, she was called on to coordinate that year's project. The theme selected was Alaskan marine mammals, appropriate because of Homer's location on the rich marine environment of Kachemak Bay. In addition, the Pratt Museum houses numerous mammal skeletons including whales, such as a beluga and a Bering Sea beaked whale. For the quilts, artist Anne Marie Holensven drew 30 simple designs, 15 for each quilt.

By this time the Pratt Museum had already established a dedicated group of volunteers. They met each Friday to share fabric and ideas, get technical advice, and help the several beginners who participated. At one of these sessions Melody was introduced to the world of rulers and rotary cutting. For the first time she was taught to use a thimble and now "can't sew a stitch without one." As a result of this project she sold her loom, gave away her yarn and knitting needles, and now has her own collection of fabrics!

Melody relates that there was joy when the quilt blocks were turned in, especially seeing the many creative interpretations – "bunched brown fabric looked like tough old walrus hide" and "shades of pink and ice blue captured the cold, icy look of a setting Arctic sun." The blocks seemed to divide naturally into two groups. After they were set together, quilting took place in one of the exhibition galleries in time for the summer tourist season. Visiting quilters added a few stitches, including some of Melody's Amish/Mennonite relatives who were visiting from Pennsylvania. All the quilters enjoyed sharing the experience of quilting together and trading stories.

The Museum sold 6,761 tickets in the fund-raising effort for 1988. This second Alaskan Marine Mammal quilt is part of the Pratt Museum's permanent collection, where it can often be seen on exhibit in the Marine Gallery. According to Betsy Webb, "It represents a sense of joy about Alaskan biological diversity and mirrors the strong Museum emphasis on ocean conservation."

The Pratt Museum's participation with "GATHERINGS: America's Quilt Heritage" is seen as perhaps being the springboard for extending their museum/community quilting involvement into an Alaskan quilt documentation project.

Much has come from quilt documentation projects, yet in many ways they are just a beginning.

One of the most important consequences has been that through project activity, materials on the proper care and storage of quilts has been disseminated. Some projects sold acid-free tissue paper and storage boxes. Almost all presented handouts on proper care or provided information about regional conservators or appraisers.

Investigating an era when quilt signatures were the exception rather than the norm, the projects' documentation and labeling process has salvaged a valuable section of history. Fortunately, today the quilts entered in shows must be identified by a fabric label, which usually includes the maker's name, and address, and the title and date of the piece. To be sure, this is a step in the right direction. For the "embroidery impaired," pens in a myriad of colors can be used to identify and permanently mark quilts. An entire subculture of fancy quilt labeling has emerged. A motivating desire for this is perhaps inspired by the thrill of finding labeled antique quilts.

The documentation projects collected vast bodies of information on both quilts and their makers. "We believe this information will serve a broad audience as it will prove invaluable to museums and historical societies as they undertake exhibits, house restorations, and begin to compile records and stories of their local residents," concludes Cheryl Kennedy of Illinois.

Documentation projects sometimes focused on helping children learn about quilts. The Arizona Project instituted a classroom education program for grades 4, 5, and 6 called QUILT-ED. Those involved produced a teachers' manual which was made available to others.[10]

"Hawaiian Quilting" a Hawaii Public Television Series, featured the Hawaiian Quilt Research Project on one of its programs. This 13-part series has aired across the country and included natural, cultural, and local history, profiles of Hawaiian quiltmakers, and lessons on making Hawaiian quilts. Arizona families were treated to PBS airings of "Arizona Quilts: Pieces of Time," the video by the Arizona Quilt Project, described by Audrey Waite as touching communities from the Grand Canyon to the valleys and deserts. She adds, "We got a wonderful glimpse into the lives of Arizonans and we like what we see."[11]

Museum and historical society collections have been enhanced by the donations of quilts by individuals who did not realize they had important textiles, or did not know how to go about donating them to the appropriate institution. As a result of interaction with project activities, museums are reassessing and upgrading their textile storage facilities.

Another important consequence has proved to be that exhibitions of the findings by the projects have brought to the public an awareness of quilts and the roles they have played in women's lives. The ordinary woman was visibly being elevated to a position of merit. United States history was reflected through the quilts that were made. Visitors were staggered by the visual and often graphic images presented by the quilts themselves. The Valentine Museum in Richmond, Virginia, reported to the Virginia Quilt Research Project that their exhibit, "Traditions and Innovation, Patchwork Quilt Designs 1840–1965," was one of the largest, longest running, and most popular shows ever in that facility's history. Attendance records at The North Carolina Museum of History were shattered by "North Carolina Quilts: Selections From the North Carolina Quilt Project."

That families have re-established contact as a result of quilt documentation projects has been an unexpected benefit. Children have been made aware of their links to past generations. A special emphasis has resulted in getting the stories from family elders before it was too late. More than a few neglected older citizens had visitors who came seeking their reminiscences. Looking at the old photo albums and recording genealogy gained a new importance. Quilts have become the focal points of family reunions. Much like the cooperative fund-raisers and friendship quilts of a previous generation, names and signatures were being collected and sewn together into quilts. Copies of family heirloom quilts have been stitched for use and display, and continue to be made today.

In the area of personal growth, there has been no limit. Men and women of the documentation projects have had their knowledge of quilts taken seriously by a public interested in history and the decorative arts. Project personnel have excelled at organization, public speaking, data management, writing, photography, fund-raising, education, business management, publicity, graphics, exhibit design, and video production. Attitudes and outlooks have shifted. "How satisfying it is to find our own perspectives changing. We are less judgmental, more accepting. Now a good quilt is not a perfect quilt; it is one whose maker's soul is seen," concludes Lois Downey a Quilt Heritage: Washington State board member.

Most of all, there has been the incredible human enrichment of new friendships and personal relationships. Virginia McElroy of the California Heritage Quilt Project speaks for many when she relates, "I think the most rewarding part of the project and what I look back at with fond memories are the relationships with the quilt owners. To share family histories and to help people realize what they had...."

The work will go on. In Michigan an outgrowth of the project has been the exhibit "African-American Quiltmaking Tradition in Michigan." Virginia plans a Phase II study of the state's contemporary quilts. As a gesture of goodwill the Georgia Project is organizing a gift of approximately 400 quilts to be given to each country's national Olympic committee and flagbearer who will participate in the Olympic Games in Atlanta in 1996. They will produce an exhibit and catalog for them in 1995.

The documentation project books are great bodies of information on both quilts and regional and state history. University presses have joined other publishers such as American Quilter's Society, Dutton, and Rutledge Hill Press in producing quilt books. The author of *Florida Quilts*, Charlotte Allen Williams recalls that, "As I look back, I realize that the part I have played in producing this book as a permanent record of our project has been very much like making a quilt."[12]

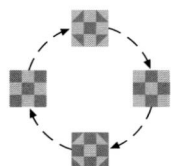

Quilts are a common denominator, a catalyst for conversation, a unifying thread in nineteenth and twentieth century United States history, especially that of women. Quilts kept bodies warm, and were used from birth to burying. They provided color and beauty to bleak homesteads and elegant mansions. They served as a tangible piece of mothers' and friends' unconditional love or admiration. They are acceptable artistic vehicles for the creative and eccentric. They are the monuments of the resourceful. Their making was a blessed excuse for the weary to sit, for the aged or infirm to feel useful, for the bored and lonely to pass the time, and they became a tool for the ambitious to be recognized. The quilt documentation projects have brought to national attention the history of both the ordinary and the extraordinary. As a result, all lives are infinitely richer. "GATHERINGS: America's Quilt Heritage" salutes them all.

Appendices

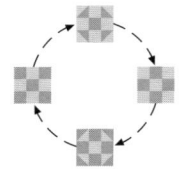

STATE QUILT PROJECT DATA
As Collected from Publications and Survey Forms

State Quilt Projects
Basic data as of February 1995

State	ALABAMA	ALASKA	ARIZONA	ARKANSAS	ARKANSAS	CALIFORNIA	COLORADO
Project Title	Alabama Quilt Search	No known Project	Arizona Quilt Project	Arkansas Quilter's Guild, Inc Project	Rogers Historical Museum Regional survey	California Heritage Quilt Project	Colorado Historical Documentation
Status	In Process		Completed	Completed	Completed	Completed	In Process
Date Begun	1987		1986	1987	1983	1983	1985
Files Open	Yes		No	No	No	No	Yes
Area	State		State	State	County (6)	State	State
Cut-off-dates on Quilts	1945		1940	1940	1936	1945	
Quilt Days	18		28	10	6	32	c.70
Number of Quilts	3000 (est.)		2774		264	3300	2700
Number of Volunteers			484		c.36	c.635	c.100
Computerization			Intended	In Process		To be decided	In Process
Computer Used							MacIntosh
Computer Program							
Housing of Raw Data	Birmingham Museum of Art Birmingham, AL		Arizona Historical Society Tempe, AZ.	Arkansas Territorial Restoration and Museum, Little Rock, AK	Rogers Historical Museum, Rogers, AK	American Quilt Research Center, LACMA Los Angeles, CA	Project Headquarters – Boulder, CO
Housing of Computerized Data	None		Arizona Historical Society Tempe, AZ	Arkansas Territorial Restoration and Museum, Little Rock, AK			Headquarters, Project Denver, CO
Restrictions on use of Data	Owner not listed		No information.	No information.	No information.	To be decided	Restricted to committee as of 11/2/93
Book	Projected 1995		Yes	Yes	Catalog	Yes	Proposed
Exhibition(s)	Yes		Yes	Yes	Yes	Yes	

State Quilt Projects
Basic data as of February 1995

State	CONNECTICUT	DELAWARE	FLORIDA	GEORGIA	HAWAII	IDAHO	ILLINOIS
Project Title	Connecticut Quilt Search Project	Delaware Folklife Project	Florida Quilt Heritage Project	Georgia Quilt Project	Hawaiian Quilt Research Project	Boise Basin Quilters Guild Registration Project	Illinois Quilt Research Project
Status	In Process	Completed	Completed	In Process	In Process	In Process	Completed
Date Begun	1991	1984	1987	1988	1990	1988	1986
Files Open	Yes	No	Yes	No	Yes	Yes	Yes
Area	State	County	State	State	State	State	State
Cut-off-dates on Quilts	1950	None	None	None	1960	None	None
Quilt Days	20 (est.)	1	43	76	17	10	30
Number of Quilts		150	5000 (est.)	8500+	800	860	15,808
Number of Volunteers	No Information	No Information	350 (est.)	"Hundreds"	162		1,000
Computerization	To be decided		None	In Process	Intended	Intended	In Process
Computer Used			Intended	IBM 386 compatible	Mac Quadra 650		
Computer Program				Alpha Four	File Pro		D Base K
Housing of Raw Data	Connecticut Historical Society Hartford, CT.	Delaware Agricultural Museum and Village Dover, DE	Museum of Florida History Tallahassee, FL	Georgia Department of Archives and History Altanta, GA	Mission Houses Museum Honolulu, HI	Idaho State Historical Library Boise, ID	Early American Museum Mahomei, IL
Housing of Computerized Data	Connecticut Historical Society Hartford, CT.		Museum of Florida History Tallahassee, FL	Georgia Department of Archives and History Altanta, GA	To be decided	Idaho State Historical Library Boise, ID	Illinois State Museum Springfield, IL
Restrictions on use of Data	Owner information only with owner's permission.	Owner information only with owner's permission.	Owner waived approval; only to qualified researchers.	Owner information only with owner's permission.	To be decided.	To be decided.	Owner information not available.
Book	Projected 1996		Yes	Projected 1996	Projected 1998		Yes
Exhibition(s)			Yes	Projected 1997	Projected 1998	Yes	Yes

State Quilt Projects
Basic data as of February 1995

State	INDIANA	IOWA	KANSAS	KENTUCKY	LOUISIANA	MAINE	MARYLAND
Project Title	Indiana Quilt Registry Project	Iowa Quilt Research Project	Kansas Quilt Project	Kentucky Quilt Project, Inc.	Louisiana Quilt Search.	Maine Quilt Heritage	Maryland Quilt Project.
Status	Completed	Completed	Completed	Completed	Completed	In Progress	In Process. No Data Received
Date Begun	1986	1988	1986	1981	1987 (Sept.)	1986	
Files Open	Yes		No	Yes	No	Yes	
Area	State	State	State	State	State	State	
Cut-off-dates on Quilts	None	1925	None	1900	1945	1960	
Quilt Days	23	26	73	12	30	25	
Number of Quilts	6400	2500 (est.)	13,107	1000 (est.)	2025 (est.)	1300	
Number of Volunteers	717	500 (est.)	300	100 (est.)	200 (est.)	181	
Computerization	In Process	Intended	Completed	None	None	In Process	
Computer Used	IBM		IBM Compatible			IBM compatible	
Computer Program	Paradox 3		D Base 3			PFS: File	
Housing of Raw Data	Indiana State Museum Indianapolis, IN	State Historical Society of Iowa Des Moines, IA.	Kansas State Historical Society Topeka, KS	University of Louisville Archives Louisville, KY	Louisiana State Department of Archives Baton Rouge, LA	New England Quilt Museum (probably) Lowell, MA	
Housing of Computerized Data	Indiana State Museum Indianapolis, IN	State Historical Society of Iowa Des Moines, IA.	Kansas Museum of History Topeka, KS			New England Quilt Museum (probably) Lowell, MA	
Restrictions on use of Data	Owner information only with owner's permission	Only if owner grants permission.	Only limited if owner restricted it.	No Information.	No Information.	Owner's name not available	
Book	Yes	No information	Yes	Yes	No	Proposed	
Exhibition(s)	Yes	Yes	Yes	Yes	Yes	Yes	

State Quilt Projects
Basic data as of February 1995

State	MASSACHUSETTS	MICHIGAN	MINNESOTA	MISSISSIPPI	MISSOURI	MONTANA	NEBRASKA
Project Title	MASS Quilts: The Massachusetts Quilt Documentation Project	Michigan Quilt Project.	Minnesota Quilt Project.	Mississippi State Historical Museum (limited)	Missouri Heritage Quilt Project.	Montana Historic Quilt Project.	Nebraska Quilt Project.
Status	In Process	Completed	In Process	Completed	Completed	In Process	Completed
Date Begun	1994	1984	1987		1983	1987	1985
Files Open	Yes	Yes	Yes		Yes	Yes	No
Area	State	State	State	Regional	State	State, regionally	State
Cut-off-dates on Quilts	1950	None	1976		1900	None	1920
Quilt Days		37	38		19	Region 5 – 12 Region 7 – No Information	28
Number of Quilts		5500	3320 (est.)		800 (est.)	Region 5 – 215 Region 7 – 175	5000 (est.)
Number of Volunteers		300 (est.)	125 (est.)		140	Region 5 – 50 Region 7 – No Information	700
Computerization	Intended	Completed	In Process		None	None	Completed
Computer Used	IBM Compatible		IBM or PC				Statistical analysis systems software; they developed.
Computer Program		Filemaker Pro	Filemaker Pro				
Housing of Raw Data	New England Quilt Museum, Lowell, MA	Michigan State University Museum, East Lansing, MI	Minnesota Historical Society, St. Paul, MN		To go to Missouri State Historical Society	Project Headquarters	Nebraska State Historical Society, Love Library Archives, U of N, Lincoln, NE
Housing of Computerized Data	New England Quilt Museum, Lowell, MA	Michigan State University Museum, East Lansing, MI	Minnesota Historical Society, St. Paul, MN				Department of Textiles, Clothing Design, U of N, Lincoln, NE
Restrictions on use of Data	Owner information restricted.	Informants may restrict access to data.	Owner's name available only if it is the quiltmaker.		To be decided.	None.	No Information
Book	Projected, 1999	Yes	Proposed	Yes	Yes		Yes
Exhibition(s)	Yes	Yes	Yes	Yes	Yes	Yes	Yes

State Quilt Projects
Basic data as of February 1995

State	NEVADA	NEW HAMPSHIRE	NEW JERSEY	NEW MEXICO	NEW MEXICO	NEW YORK	NORTH CAROLINA
Project Title	Nevada State Heritage Quilt Project.	New Hampshire Quilt Documentation Project.	Heritage Quilt Project of New Jersey	Survey of Hispanic Quiltmaking Tradition in Taos County.	New Mexico Heritage Quilt Search	New York Quilt Project	North Carolina Quilt Project
Status	In Process	In Process	Completed	Completed	Completed	Completed	Completed
Date Begun	1987	1988	1986	1991	1987	1985	1985
Files Open	No	Yes	Future	Yes	No	Yes	No
Area	State	State	State	County	State	State	State
Cut-off-dates on Quilts	None	1940	1950	None	1945	1940	1976
Quilt Days	19	16	32	6	22	45	72
Number of Quilts	3000 (est.)	969	2200 (est.)	187	950	6000+	10,106
Number of Volunteers	250 (est.)	120	350	7	180	1800–2000	
Computerization	In Process	In Process	Intended	None	None	In Process	In Process
Computer Used							IBM compatible
Computer Program						MAFA Professional File	D Base III
Housing of Raw Data	Project Headquarters; Nevada Historical Society Reno, NV.	Currently, project hands	Rutgers University Special Collections and Archives New Brunswick, NJ	Director's Home	Currently Director's Home	Museum of American Folk Art New York, NY	Museum of History Raleigh, NC
Housing of Computerized Data		Currently, project hands	Rutgers University Special Collections and Archives New Brunswick, NJ			Museum of American Folk Art New York, NY	Museum of History Raleigh, NC
Restrictions on use of Data	Owner information not available.	Owner information not available.	Owner information available only with written permission.	No information.	Not available at this time.	Available only to qualified researchers.	No Information.
Book	Projected 1995	Projected	Yes	Yes	Projected 1996	Yes	Yes
Exhibition(s)	Proposed		Yes		Yes	Yes	Yes

State Quilt Projects
Basic data as of February 1995

State	NORTH DAKOTA	OHIO**	OKLAHOMA	OREGON	PENNSYLVANIA	PENNSYLVANIA**	PENNSYLVANIA**
Project Title	North Dakota Quilt Project.	Ohio Quilt Research Project.	Oklahoma Quilt Heritage Project.	Columbia-Willamette Quilt Study Group Survey (limited).	Oral Traditionas Project	Adams County Quilt Project	Berks County Quilt Harvest
Status	In Process	Completed	Completed	Completed	Completed	Completed	Completed
Date Begun	1986	1984	1984		1973		
Files Open	No				Yes		
Area	State	State	State		Counties (15)	County	County
Cut-off-dates on Quilts	1969		1940		1940		1940
Quilt Days	32	51	19		20		9
Number of Quilts	3521	7000	4000+		3500 (est.)		1400
Number of Volunteers	387+	No Information	502		56		145
Computerization	Intended	In Process	Intended		None		
Computer Used	IBM compatible						
Computer Program							
Housing of Raw Data	Quilter's Guild of North Dakota Fargo, ND State Historical Society State Archives Bismarck, ND.	Ohio Historical Society Division of Archives & Manuscripts, Columbus, OH	Oklahoma State Historical Museum Oklahoma City, OK		Union County Historical Society Lewisburg, PA		
Housing of Computerized Data	No Information	Ohio Historical Society Division of Archives & Manuscripts, Columbus, OH	To go to Oklahoma State Historical Museum Oklahoma City, OK				
Restrictions on use of Data	No information.	Owner information is confidential.	Owner information restricted.		Owner information not available.		
Book	Catalog	Yes	Yes	Yes	Yes	Yes	Catalog
Exhibition(s)	Yes	Yes	Yes		Yes	Yes	Yes

** Data from published sources only: no questionnaire received.

State Quilt Projects
Basic data as of February 1995

State	PENNSYLVANIA	PENNSYLVANIA	RHODE ISLAND	SOUTH CAROLINA	SOUTH DAKOTA	TENNESSEE	TEXAS**
Project Title	Goschenhoppen Quilt Round Up	Lancaster County Quilt Harvest	Rhode Island Quilt Documentation Project	South Carolina Quilt History Project	No known project.	Quilts of Tennessee	Texas Quilt Search
Status	Completed	Completed	In Process	Completed		Completed	Completed
Date Begun	1989	1987	1992	1983		1983	1984
Files Open	Yes	Yes	Yes	No		Yes	
Area	Region	County	State	County (12)		State	State
Cut-off-dates on Quilts	1950	1946	1950	1970		1930	1936
Quilt Days	18	11	11	37 (est.)		30	27
Number of Quilts	1553	829	684	1300 (est.)		2020	3500
Number of Volunteers	80	80	50	37		1000 (est.)	
Computerization	Intended	In Process	In Process	Intended		Intended	No information
Computer Used		IBM compatible	MacIntosh				
Computer Program		Enable Data	Filemaker Pro				
Housing of Raw Data	Goschenhoppen Folklife Museum and Library	Heritage Center Lancaster, PA	University of Rhode Island, Dept. of Textiles, Fashion, Merchandising and Design Kingston, RI	Folk Art Archives, McKissick Museum of South Carolina Columbia, SC		Tennessee State Library and Archives Nashville, TN	Texas Quilt Library and Archives
Housing of Computerized Data	To go to Goschenhoppen Folklife Museum and Library	Heritage Center Lancaster, PA	University of Rhode Island, Dept. of Textiles, Fashion, Merchandising and Design Kingston, RI	McKissick Museum of South Carolina Columbia, SC			
Restrictions on use of Data	No information.	Owner information confidential.	Owner information restricted.	Owner information. only by appointment.		Limited to scholarly research.	No information.
Book	Yes		Projected 1996	Yes		Yes	Yes
Exhibition(s)	Yes	Yes	Yes	Yes		Yes	Yes

** Data from published sources only: no questionnaire received.

State Quilt Projects
Basic data as of February 1995

State	TEXAS	UTAH	VERMONT	VIRGINIA	VIRGINIA	WASHINGTON	WASHINGTON DC
Project Title	Texas Quilt Heritage Society Project	Utah Quilt Heritage Corporation	Vermont Quiltsearch	Virginia Quilt Research Project	The Virginia Search – Northern Virginia	Quilt Heritage: Washington State	"Made in DC" Quilt Search, Inc.
Status	Completed	No Data Received	Completed	In Process	Completed	In Process	Completed
Date Begun	1984		1988	1987	1985 (May)	1988	1987
Files Open	No		Yes	Yes	Yes	Yes	No
Area	State		State	State	Regional	State	City
Cut-off-dates on Quilts	None		1960	1976	1985	1970	None
Quilt Days	18		20	30	12	100 (est.)	13
Number of Quilts	2200		1100+	3412	1000	7500 (est.)	415
Number of Volunteers	183		125	700 (est.)	30	1200	20
Computerization	None		None	Intended	None	In Process	None
Computer Used				IBM		IBM	
Computer Program				Developing own program		D Base IV	
Housing of Raw Data	To be decided		Vermont Quilt Festival Northfield, VT	Virginia Quilt Museum (use project address)	Fairfax County (VA) Park Authority Division of Historic Preservation Fairfax, VA	Washington State Historical Society Tacoma, WA	To go to Historical Society of Washington, D.C.
Housing of Computerized Data				Valentine Museum, proposed VA Quilt Museum or Virginia Historical Society		Yakima Valley Museum Yakima, WA	
Restrictions on use of Data	To be decided		Owner information confidential.	Owner information confidential.	Owner information confidential.	Owner information restricted.	No information.
Book	Yes		Yes, also catalogs	Projected 1996	Catalog	No	No
Exhibition(s)	Yes		Yes	Yes	Yes	Yes	Yes

State Quilt Projects
Basic data as of February 1995

State	**WEST VIRGINIA**	**WISCONSIN**	**WYOMING**
Project Title	West Virginia Heritage Quilt Search, Inc.	Wisconsin Quilt History Project, Inc.	No known project
Status	In Process	In Process	
Date Begun	1990	1988	
Files Open	Yes	Yes	
Area	State	State	
Cut-off-dates on Quilts	1940	1950	
Quilt Days	42	47	
Number of Quilts	4000 (est.)	6000+	
Number of Volunteers			
Computerization	In Process	In process	
Computer Used	DOS	IBM compatible	
Computer Program	Designed by Walt Kordek	Self authored	
Housing of Raw Data	WV Dept of Archives and History, Charleston, WV	To be decided	
Housing of Computerized Data	WV Dept of Archives and History, Charleston, WV	To be decided	
Restrictions on use of Data	Owner information restricted.	Owner information restricted.	
Book	Projected 1997	Projected 1998	
Exhibition(s)	To coincide with book publication.	No Information	

State Contacts
Addresses for State & Regional Projects

Alabama
Alabama Quilt Search Project
Gail Trechsel & Bryding Adams
Birmingham Museum of Art
2000 8th Ave. N
Birmingham, AL 35203
205-254-2566

Arizona
Arizona Quilt Project
PO Box 5062
Mesa, AZ 85211
602-282-7311

Arkansas
Historic Ozark Quilts & Quiltmakers
Gaye Bland
Rogers Historical Museum
322 S. 2nd St.
Rogers, AR 72756
501-621-1154

Arkansas
Arkansas Quilter's Guild, Inc.
No current address

California
California Heritage Quilt Project
Celia LoPinto
Box 3254
San Rafael, CA 94912
415-928-3261

Colorado
Colorado Historical Documentation
c/o Colorado Quilting Council
PO Box 2056
Arvada, CO 80002

Connecticut
Connecticut Quilt Search Project
PO Box 926
New Haven, CT 06504

Delaware
Delaware Folklife Project
Jennifer Dolde
Delaware Agricultural Museum
866 N. Dupont Hwy
Dover, DE 19901
302-734-1618

Florida
Florida Quilt Heritage Project
Charlotte A. Williams
419 North Ride
Tallahassee, FL 32303
904-385-2602

Georgia
Georgia Quilt Project
Box 34
Norcross, GA 30091-0034

Hawaii
Gussie Bento
Hawaiian Quilt Research Project
PO Box 491
Kailua, HI 96734
808-235-2372

Idaho
Boise Basin Quilters Guild
    Registration Project
PO Box 2206
Boise, ID 83701

Illinois
Illinois Quilt Research Project
Cheryl Kennedy
Early American Museum
P.O. Box 1040
Mahomet, IL 61853
217-586-2612

Indiana
Indiana Quilt Registry Project
Indiana State Museum
202 N. Alabama Street
Indianapolis, IN 46204
317-232-5607

Iowa
Martha Henrichs
Iowa Quilt Research Project
5730 Allison
Des Moines, IA 50310

Kansas
Kansas Quilt Project
Eleanor Malone
8126 Mockingbird Ln.
Wichita, KS 67207
316-683-6730

Kentucky
The Kentucky Quilt Project, Inc.
PO Box 6251
Louisville, KY 40206
502-587-6721

Louisiana
Louisiana Quilt Search
823 Robinson Pl.
Shreveport, LA 71104
318-425-3851

Maine
Maine Quilt Heritage
6 Mechanic St.
Bath, ME 04530
207-443-9076

Maryland
Maryland Quilt Project
PO Box 1726
Glen Burnie, MD 21060
410-761-9660

Massachusetts
MASS Quilts: The Massachusetts
    Quilt Documentation Project
Sandra G. Munsey
12 Old Mill Rd.
Norfolk, MA 02056

Michigan
Michigan Quilt Project
Michigan Traditional Arts Program
Michigan State University Museum
E. Lansing, MI 48824-1045
517-355-2370

Minnesota
Minnesota Quilt Project
11909 Baypoint Dr.
Burnsville, MN 55337
612-890-7299

Mississippi
(limited regional survey)
Mary Lohrenz
Mississippi State Historical Museum
PO Box 571
Jackson, MS 39205-0571
601-359-6929

Missouri
Missouri Heritage Quilt Project
1108 Sunset Ln.
Columbia, MO 65203-2253
314-449-1602

Montana
Montana Historic Quilt Project,
    Region 5
Joyce Morgan
2145 Lomas Dr.
Bozeman, MT 59715

Montana
Montana Historic Quilt Project,
    Region 7
Karen Stanton
Box G
Hardin, MT 59034

Montana
Montana Historic Quilt Project,
    Region 1
Shirley Barrett
1045 Conrad Dr.
Kalispell, MT 59901

Nebraska
Nebraska Quilt Project
Frankie Best
1820 St. James Rd.
Lincoln, NE 68506
402-488-1820

Nevada
Nevada State Heritage Quilt Project
PO Box 9524
Reno, NV 89507

New Hamshire
New Hamshire Quilt
   Documentation Project
62 Mammoth Rd.
Londonderry, NH 03053
603-434-1596

New Jersey
The Heritage Quilt Project of
   New Jersey, Inc.
Barbara Schaffer
PO Box 341
Livingston, NJ 07039
201-994-3688

New Mexico
Survey of the Hispanic Quiltmaking
   Tradition in Taos County
Dorothy Zopf
Box 424
Arroyo Seco, NM 87514
505-776-2449

New Mexico
Bonita Ensenberger
New Mexico Heritage Quilt Search
3848 Pitt St. NE
Albuquerque, NM 87111
505-296-1719

New York
New York Quilt Project
Phyllis Tepper
Museum of American Folk Art
61 West 62nd Street
New York, NY 10023-7015
212-977-7176

North Carolina
North Carolina Quilt Project
Ruth H. Roberson
3406 Ogburn Court
Durham, NC 27705

North Dakota
North Dakota Quilt Project
1450 S. 8th St.
Fargo, ND 58103
701-293-7395

Ohio
Ohio Quilt Research Project
Ellice Ronsheim
Ohio Historical Society Museum
1982 Velma Ave.
Columbus, OH 43211
614-297-2649

Oklahoma
Oklahoma Quilt Heritage Project
Central Oklahoma Quilters Guild
PO Box 23916
Oklahoma City, OK 73123

Oregon
Quilt Contest Survey
Mary Cross
Columbia-Willamette
   Quilt Study Group
805 NW Skyline Court
Portland, OR 97229

Pennsylvania
Adams County Quilt Project
PO Box 3172
Gettysburg, PA 17325

Pennsylvania
Oral Traditions Project
Union County Courthouse
S. Second & St. Louis Sts.
Lewisburg, PA 17837
717-524-8666

Pennsylvania
Goschenhoppen Quilt Round Up
PO Box 476
Green Lane, PA 18054
215-234-8953

Pennsylvania
Lancaster County Quilt Harvest
Phyllis Thompson
Heritage Center of Lancaster County
13 W. King St.
Lancaster, PA 17603
717-299-6440

Pennsylvania
Berks County Quilt Harvest
Alison DuPont
940 Center Ave.
Reading, PA 19601

Rhode Island
Rhode Island Quilt
   Documentation Project
Linda Welters
Dept. of Textiles, Fashion,
   Merchandising, & Design
303 Quinn Hall
University of Rhode Island
Kingston, RI 02883
401-792-4574

South Carolina
South Carolina Quilt Project
Laurel Horton
302 East S. 3rd St.
Seneca, SC 29678

Tennessee
Quilts of Tennessee
Bets Ramsey
322 Pine Ridge Rd.
Chattanooga, TN 37405-3430
615-265-4300

Texas
Texas Quilt Search Project
Texas Heritage Quilt Society
No current address

Texas
Texas Quilt Search
Quilt Market
14520 Memorial #54
Houston, TX 77079

Utah
Utah Quilt Heritage Corporation
1276 W. 6400 South
Salt Lake City, UT 84123
801-266-0334

Vermont
Vermont Quiltsearch
PO Box 349
Northfield, VT 05663
802-485-7092

Virginia
The Virginia Quilt Research Project
1205 Hillcrest Dr.
Harrisonburg, VA 22801
703-432-1192

Virginia
The Virginia Search –
   Northern Virginia
1604 Palm Springs Dr.
Vienna, VA 22182
703-938-3246

Washington
Sally Ambrose
Quilt Heritage Washington State
PO Box 536
Leavenworth, WA 98826
509-548-7472

Washington DC
"Made in DC" Quilt Search
Sue Hannan
5801 Nebraska Ave. NW
Washington, DC 20015
202-966-9178

West Virginia
West Virginia Heritage
   Quilt Search, Inc.
c/o Margaret Meador
Rt 6 Box 109
Princeton, WV 24740
304-425-6774

Wisconsin
Wisconsin Quilt History Project, Inc.
PO Box 174
Thiensville, WI 53092

Endnotes

CHAPTER ONE

1. Barbara Brackman, "Crescendo of Quilts," *Americana*, (June 1990), p. 38.
2. Joyce Joines Newman, *North Carolina Country Quilts: Regional Variations*, n.p.
3. Jonathan Holstein and John Finley, *Kentucky Quilts 1800-1900*, (New York: Pantheon Books, 1982), preface, pp. 15-20.
4. Phone conversation with author, October, 1993.
5. Cheryl Kennedy, letter dated 1/30/93 to Gatherings Project.
6. Katy Christopherson, "Beyond the Kentucky Quilt Project." *Lady's Circle Patchwork Quilts*, (April / May 1987), p. 39.
7. Kari Ronning. "The Nebraska Quilt Project Quilt." Paper prepared for Gatherings Project.

CHAPTER TWO

1. For more complete information, see Mary Cross, "Reflections on an Oregon Quilt Contest," in *Bits and Pieces*, pp. 100-109.

CHAPTER THREE

1. See Alan G. Keyser, "All In and All Done?: The Pennsylvania Vendue," *On the Cutting Edge*, pp. 42-47.
1a. For further information, see Mary Lohrenz and Anita Stamper, *Mississippi Homespun: Nineteenth Century Textiles and the Women who Made Them*, and Mary Lohrenz, "Two Lives Intertwined on a Tennessee Plantation: Textile Production as Recorded in the Diary of Narcissa L. Erwin Black."
2. Merikay Waldvogel, *Soft Covers For Hard Times*, (Nashville: Rutledge Hill Press, 1990), p. 38.
3. Merikay Waldvogel and Barbara Brackman. *Patchwork Souvenirs of the 1933 World's Fair*, Nashville: Rutledge Hill Press, 1993), p. 11.
4. Broadus Mitchell, *William Gregg: Factory Master of the Old South*, (Chapel Hill: University of North Carolina Press, 1928).
5. *Ibid.*, p. 15.
6. Laurel Horton, *Patterns In History: 19th Century Quilts*, n.p.
7. Mitchell, op.cit., p. 256.
8. Roland Freeman, *Something to Keep You Warm*, n.p.
9. Ricky Clark, "Sisters, Saints, and Sewing Societies: Quiltmakers' Communities," *Quilts in Community: Ohio's Traditions*, p. 155.
10. See "Arizona Quilter of the Year: Emma Andres," *Quilter's Newsletter* (April, 1984), Janet Carruth and Laurene Sinema, "Emma M. Andres and Her Six Grand Old Characters," and Helen Young Frost and Pam Knight Stevenson, *Grand Endeavors: Vintage Arizona Quilts and Their Makers*.
11. Mary Washington Clarke, *Kentucky Quilts and Their Makers*, (Lexington: University of Kentucky Press, 1976), p. 77.
12. Emily Ellen Scharf, *Famous Saddle Horses*.
13. See Helen Young Frost and Pam Knight Stevenson, *Grand Endeavors: Vintage Arizona Quilts and Their Makers*, pp. 18-22, Catrien Ross Laetz, "San Bernadino Ranch," *Arizona Highways*, (Oct 1986), pp. 3-11, and Reba N. Wells, "Cora Viola Howell Slaughter: Southern Arizona Ranchwoman," *Journal of Arizona History*, (Winter 1989), pp. 391-416.
15. Barbara Brackman et al., *Kansas Quilts & Quilters*, (Lawrence: University of Kansas Press, 1993), p. 123.
16. Barbara Brackman, *Midcentury Masterpieces: Quilts in Emporia, Kansas 1935-1950*, p. 7.
17. Henry Dreyfuss, *Symbol Sourcebook*, (New York: McGraw Hill, 1972), p. 127.
18. Newsletter "Pieces," Arizona Quilt Project, Issue Six, Spring 1989.
19. Rachel Cochran et al., *New Jersey Quilts– 1777 to 1950*, (Paducah, KY: American Quilter's Society, 1992), p.99.
20. Brackman et al., op. cit. p. 135.
21. Elizabeth Akana, letter to author, October, 1993.
22. Information and statistics supplied by the NAMES Project Foundation, 310 Townsend Street, Suite 310, San Francisco, CA 94107.

CHAPTER FOUR

1. Information on campaign ribbons provided by Julie Powell.
    For more information see Julie Powell's article "Political and Campaign Textiles," *On the Cutting Edge*, pp. 26–33.
2. Information from "Memories of the Harrington Fair" by Sharon Morgan for *The Delmarva Farmer*, July 24, 1990.
3. Jeannette Lasansky, "The Role of Haps in Central Pennsylvania's 19th and 20th Century Quiltmaking Traditions," *Uncoverings 1985*, pp. 85–93.
4. *Ibid.*
5. Aletha Conner, "Oklahoma History Quilt," p. 5.
6. Carrie Hall and Rose Kretsinger, *The Romance of the Patchwork Quilt in America*, (New York: Bonanza Books, 1935), p. 39.
7. Conner, op.cit., p. 5.
8. Information taken from "Anecdotes of Bessie Lewis' Quilts" edited by Mrs. J. K. Cockrell, Sr.

CHAPTER FIVE

1. Bets Ramsey and Merikay Waldvogel, *The Quilts of Tennessee*, (Nashville: Rutledge Hill Press, 1986), p. 94.
2. Ellice Ronsheim "From Bolt to Bed," *Quilts in Community: Ohio's Traditions*, p.56.
3. Kari Ronning. "The Lincoln Quilters Guild Research Project Quilt." Paper prepared for Gatherings Project.
4. Merikay Waldvogel. Letter to Paul Pilgrim and Gerald Roy, curators for Gatherings, July 26, 1993.
5. Merikay Waldvogel, "Searching for Sarah Berry and Her Quilts," *Quilters Newsletter Magazine*, (June, 1994), p. 25.
6. Information from research paper. "Alabama Gunboat" by E. Bryding Adams, and Bryding Adams Henley, "Gunboat Quilts: The Alabama Women's Gunboat Fund," *Alabama Heritage*, (Spring, 1988).
7. Dorothy Zopf, "The Joys of Tradition," *Toas Magazine*, (Nov / Dec 1991), p.20.
8. For more information see "The Quilts of One New Jersey Family" in Rachel Cochran et al., op. cit., pp. 38–42.
10. Pam Knight Stevenson, "Quilting in the Classroom, *Quilters Newsletter Magazine*, (Nov / Dec 1988).
11. Audrey Waite in Arizona Quilt Project newsletter, *Pieces* (Fall 1992).
12. Charlotte Allen Williams, *Florida Quilts*, (Gainesville: University of Florida Press, 1992), preface.

Bibliography

This listing includes publications resulting from state or regional quilt survey projects. (each marked by an asterisk) and other publications providing related information If a publication is related to a specific state and the title does not make that clear, the state name appears in parenthesis at the end of the entry.

*Adams County Quilt Documentation Committee. *The Hands That Made Them: Quilts of Adams County, Pennsylvania*. Camp Hill, PA: Adams County Quilt Project committee, 1993.

Akana, Elizabeth. "Ku`u Hae Aloha," *The Quilt Digest Press 2*. San Francisco, CA: Kiracofe and Kile, 1984: 77–77.

*Arkansas Quilter's Guild, Inc. *Arkansas Quilts, Arkansas Warmth*. Paducah, KY: American Quilter's Society, 1987.

*Atkins, Jacqueline M., and Phyllis A. Tepper. *New York Beauties: Quilts from the Empire State*. New York, NY: Dutton Studio Books, 1992.

"Arizona Quilter of the Year: Emma Andres." *Quilter's Newsletter Magazine* (April 1984): 8-9.

Barber, Rita Barrow. *Somewhere in Between: Quilts and Quilters of Illinois*. Paducah, KY: American Quilter's Society, 1986.

Brackman Barbara. *Clues in the Calico: A Guide to Identifying and Dating Antique Quilts*. McLean, VA: EPM Publications, Inc., 1989.

Brackman Barbara. "Crescendo of Quilts." *Americana Magazine* (May / June 1990): 35–39.

Brackman Barbara. *Encyclopedia of Pieced Quilt Patterns*. Paducah, KY: American Quilter's Society, 1993.

*Brackman, Barbara et al. *Kansas Quilts and Quilters*. Lawrence, KS: University of Kansas Press, 1993.

Brackman, Barbara. *Midcentury Masterpieces: Quilts in Emporia, Kansas 1935-1950*. Wichita Art Museum.

*Bresenhan, Karoline Patterson and Nancy O'Bryant Puentes. *Lone Stars, A Legacy of Texas Quilts, 1836-1936, Vol. I*. Austin, TX: University of Texas Press, 1986.

*Bresenhan, Karoline Patterson and Nancy O'Bryant Puentes. *Lone Stars, A Legacy of Texas Quilts, 1936-1986, Vol. II*. Austin, TX: University of Texas Press, 1990.

Carruth, Janet and Laurene Sinema. "Emma M. Andres and Her Six Grand Old Characters." In *Uncoverings 1990*, San Francisco, CA: American Quilt Study Group: 88–106.

*Carter, Hazel. *Virginia Quilts, First Search for Virginia-made Quilts, Beginning in Northern Virginia, 1987*. Vienna, VA: The Continental Quilt Congress, 1987.

Christopherson, Katy. "Beyond the Kentucky Quilt Project." *Lady's Circle Patchwork Quilts* (April / May 1987): 38–39.

*Clark, Ricky, George W. Knepper, and Ellice Ronsheim. *Quilts in Community: Ohio Traditions*. Nashville, TN: Rutledge Hill Press, 1991.

Clarke, Mary Washington. *Kentucky Quilts and Their Makers*. Lexington, KY: University Press of Kentucky, 1976.

*Cleveland, Richard L. and Donna Bister. *Plain and Fancy, Vermont's People and Their Quilts*. San Francisco, CA: The Quilt Digest Press, 1991.

*Cochran, Rachel, et al. *New Jersey Quilts – 1777 to 1950: Contributions to an American Tradition*. Paducah, KY: American Quilter's Society, 1992.

Columbia-Willamette Quilt Study Group. *Women's Work: A Study of Quilts*. Portland, OR: Columbia-Willamette Quilt Study Group, Mary Cross, ed., 1984.

Conner, Aletha Caldwell. *The Oklahoma History Quilt*. Oklahoma Historical Society, 1935.

*Crews, Patricia Cox, and Ronald C. Naugle, eds. *Nebraska Quilts and Quiltmakers*. Lincoln and London, NE: University of Nebraska Press, 1991.

Cross, Mary. "Reflections on an Oregon Quilt Contest." *In Bits and Pieces: Textile Traditions*, Lasansky, ed. Lewisburg, PA: Oral Traditions Project, 1991: 100–109.

Cross, Mary Bywater, *Treasures in the Trunk: Quilts of the Oregon Trail*. Nashville, TN: Rutledge Hill Press, 1993.

Davis, Carolyn O'Bagy. *Quilted All Day: The Prairie Journals of Ida Chambers Melugin (1867-1955)*. Tucson, AZ: Sanpete Publications, 1993. (Arizona)

Dreyfuss, Henry. *Symbol Sourcebook*. New York, NY: McGraw Hill Book Co., 1972.

*Eanes, Ellen Fickling, et al. *North Carolina Quilts*. Chapel Hill, NC: University of North Carolina Press, 1988.

*Elbert, E. Duane, and Rachel Kamm Elbert. *History from the Heart: Quilt Paths across Illinois*. Nashville, TN: Rutledge Hill Press, 1993.

Fox, Sandi: *Quilts in Utah: A Reflection of the Western Experience*. Salt Lake City, UT: Salt Lake Art Center, 1981.

Freeman, Roland. *Something To Keep You Warm*. Jackson, MS: Mississippi Department of Archives and History, June 14- August 9, 1981.

*Frost, Helen Young, and Pam Knight Stephenson. *Grand Endeavors: Vintage Arizona Quilts and Their Makers*. Flagstaff, AZ: Northland Publishing, 1992.

Hall, Carrie A., and Rose G. Kretsinger. *The Romance of the Patchwork Quilt in America*. New York: Bonanza Books, 1935.

*Harnden, Jane Amstatz, and Pamela Frazee Woolbright, eds. *Oklahoma Heritage Quilts: A Sampling of Quilts Made in or Brought to Oklahoma before 1940*. Paducah, KY: American Quilter's Society, 1990.

*Havig, Bettina. *Missouri Heritage Quilts*. Paducah, KY: American Quilter's Society, 1986.

Henley, Bryding Adams. "*Gunboat Quilts: The Alabama Women's Gunboat Fund.*" Alabama Heritage (Spring 1988): 14–25.

Hoffman, Victoria. *Quilts, A Window to the Past.* North Andover, MA: The Museum of American Textile History, 1991.

*Holstein, Jonathan, and John Finley. *Kentucky Quilts, 1800–1900.* New York, NY: Pantheon Books, 1982.

Horton, Laurel. *Patterns in History: Nineteenth Century Quilts.* The Charleston Museum, undated.

*Horton, Laurel, and Lynn Robertson Myers. *Social Fabric: South Carolina's Traditional Quilts.* Columbia, SC: University of South Carolina, McKissick Museum, 1986.

*Indiana Quilt Registry Project. *Quilts of Indiana: Crossroads of Memories.* Bloomington and Indianapolis: Indiana University Press, 1991.

Keyser, Alan G., "All In and All Done?: The Pennsylvania Vendue." *In On the Cutting Edge,* Lasansky, ed.: 42–47.

Laetz, Catrien Ross. "San Bernadino Ranch." *Arizona Highways* (October 1986): 3–11.

Lasansky, Jeannette, ed. *Bits and Pieces: Textile Traditions.* Lewisburg, PA: Oral Traditions Project, 1991. (Pennsylvania)

*Lasansky, Jeannette. *In the Heart of Pennsylvania: 19th and 20th Century Quiltmaking Traditions.* Lewisburg, PA: Oral Traditions Project, 1985.

Lasansky, Jeannette, ed. *In the Heart of Pennsylvania, Symposium Papers.* Lewisburg, PA: Oral Traditions Project, 1986.

Lasansky, Jeannette, ed. *On the Cutting Edge: Textile Collectors, Collections, and Traditions.* Lewisburg, PA: Oral Traditions Project, 1993. (Pennsylvania)

*Lasansky, Jeannette. *Pieced By Mother: Over 100 Years of Quiltmaking Traditions.* Lewisburg, PA: Oral Traditions Project, 1987. (Pennsylvania)

Lasansky, Jeannette. "The Role of Haps in Century Pennsylvania's 19th and 20th Century Quiltmaking Traditions." *Uncoverings 1985.* Mill Valley, CA: American Quilt Study Group: 85–93.

*Laury, Jean Ray, and California Heritage Quilt Project. *Ho For California!: Pioneer Women and Their Quilts.* New York, NY: E.P. Dutton, 1990.

Laury, Jean Ray, and Linda Reuther. *Sarah Berry Quilts.* Fresno Art Museum, September 7– November 14, 1993.

Lohrenz, Mary Edna, and Anita Miller Stamper. *Mississippi Homespun: Nineteenth–Century Textiles and the Women Who Made Them.* Jackson, MS: Mississippi Department of Archives and History, 1989.

Lohrenz, Mary. "Two Lives Intertwined on a Tennessee Plantation: Textile Production as Recorded in the Diary of Narcissa L. Erwin Black." University of Southern Mississippi: *The Southern Quarterly,* Fall 1988: 73–93.

*Luster, Michael. *Stitches in Time: A Legacy of Ozark Quilts.* Rogers, AR: Rogers Historical Museum, 1986.

*MacDowell, Marsha, and Ruth E. Fitzgerald. *Michigan Quilts: 150 Years of Textile Traditions.* East Lansing, MI: Michigan State University Museums, 1987.

McLachlem, Diana. *A Common Thread, Quilts in the Yakima Valley.* Yakima, WA: Yakima Valley Museum and Historical Association, 1985. (Washington State)

Mitchell, Broadus. *William Gregg: Factory Master of the Old South.* Chapel Hill: University of North Carolina Press, 1928.

North Carolina Country Quilts. Chapel Hill, NC: The Ackland Art Museum, 1978.

Prairie Windmill Quilt History and Research Chapter, National Quilting Association. *Quilts of the South Texas Plains.* Lubbock, TX: Texas Tech University, 1986.

Powell, Julie. "Quilted Ballots: Political and Campaign Textiles." *In On the Cutting Edge,* Lasansky, ed.: 26–33.

*Ramsey, Bets, and Merikay Waldvogel. *The Quilts of Tennessee: Images of Domestic Life Prior to 1930.* Nashville, TN: Rutledge Hill Press, 1986.

*Roan, Nancy and Donald Roan. *Lest I Shall Be Forgotten: Anecdotes and Traditions of Quilts.* Green Lane, PA: Goschenhoppen Historians, Inc., 1993.

Scharf, Emily Ellen. *Famous Saddle Horses.*

Schorsch, Anita. *Plain & Fancy: Country Quilts of the Pennsylvania-Germans.* New York, NY: Sterling Publications Company, Inc. 1992.

Silber, Julie and Eve Wheatcroft Granick. *Amish Quilts of Lancaster Country.* San Francisco, CA: Esprit de Corps, 1990. (Pennsylvania)

Stevenson, Pam Knight. "Quilting in the Classroom." *Quilter's Newsletter Magazine* (November / December 1988): 26–28.

*Texas Heritage Quilt Society Book Committee. *Texas Quilts, Texas Treasures.* Paducah, KY: American Quilter's Society, 1986.

The Thread That Remains: Patterns From Iowa's Past: May 13 – September 2, 1990.

Twelker, Nancyann Johnson. *Women and Their Quilts, A Washington Centennial Tribute.* Bothell, WA: That Patchwork Place, 1988.

Waldvogel, Merikay, and Barbara Brackman. *Patchwork Souvenirs of the 1933 World's Fair.* Nashville: Rutledge Hill Press, 1993.

Waldvogel, Merikay. "Searching For Sarah Berry and Her Quilts." *Quilter's Newsletter Magazine* (June 1994): 24-25.

Waldvogel, Merikay. *Soft Covers for Hard Times: Quiltmaking and the Great Depression.* Nashville: Rutledge Hill Press, 1990.

Wells, Reba N., "Cora Viola Howell Slaughter: Southern Arizona Ranchwoman." Journal of Arizona History (Winter 1989): 391–416.

"What Mother Did, I Did Too": Kansas Quilt Traditions. Topeka, KA: Kansas State Historical Society, 1991.

*Williams, Charlotte Allen. *Florida Quilts.* Gainesville, FL: University of Florida Press, 1992.

Zopf, Dorothy R. "The Hispanic Traditions of Quiltmaking in Taos County, New Mexico." *In On The Cutting Edge,* Lasansky, ed.: 102–107.

Zopf, Dorothy. "The Joys of Tradition." *Taos Magazine,* (Nov / Dec, 1991), 20–21.

Index

QUILT NAMES OR PATTERNS

Album	56
An American Family	128
Appliqué Quilt	160
Appliqué Quilt	182
Arizona Commemorative	104
Baltimore Bride's Quilt	140
Basket Medallion	164
Blue and White Scrap Quilt	102
Blue Patchwork Cross	176
Box Car Quilt (Wild Goose Chase)	74
Broken Star	175
Brown Goose	72
Carnation Flour Sack Quilt	168
Champion Ribbons Quilt	152
Chester Dare Crazy Quilt	108
Child's Quilt	186
Chintz Appliqué Medallion	138
Crazy Quilt	134
Delectable Mountains	156
Double X	58
Double Z	72
Dove in the Window	64
Escher's Triangles #52	28
Feather Plumes with Coxcombs	114
Feathered Star Variation	132
Flower Basket Appliqué Quilt	92
Flying Geese	78
Four Flower Pots Appliqué	49
French Smoothing Iron	94
Friendship Quilt	106
Garden #4, The	118
Geometry Sampler	40
Grandmother's Flower Garden Quilt	112
Grandmother's Garden	34
Hap	162
Hawaiian Flag Quilt	42
Hearts and Gizzards	36
Hydrangea Quilt	178
Illinois Sampler Quilt	66
Irish Chain	30
Kukui O Lono (Lamp of Lono)	126
Little Red Schoolhouse	99
Lone Star with Broderie Perse #12	192
Love Apple and Rose	198
Lucy's Baskets	32
Map of U.S.A.	52
Marine Mammal Quilt	200
Masonic Emblem Quilt	81
Memories of the Nebraska Quilt Project	18
Milwaukee's Own (Mississippi Oak Leaf)	194
Miracle Quilt of Democracy	116
Morning Glory Quilt	180
NAMES Project AIDS Memorial Quilt	136
Navy Yard Quilt Top	170
Nine Patch	122
Nine-Patch on Point	190
Oklahoma History Quilt	166
Orange Peel Crib Quilt	96
Pan American Exposition Quilt	76
Pillow Cover	148
Pomegranate Quilt	196
Postage Stamp Quilt	68
Prairie Star	82
Printed Flannel Flag Quilt	113
Puff Quilt	136
Relampago (Lightning)	188
Reverse Appliqué	50
Sawtooth Square Variation	88
Say Cheese	44
Schoolhouse	100
Schoolhouse Scrap Quilt	38
Scotch-Irish Quilt	184
Secession Quilt	146
Setting Sun Quilt	172
Signature Quilt	142
Silk and Velvet Crazy Quilt	54
Silk Mosaic	62
Slave Chain	90
Star of Bethlehem	80
Sunflower Quilt	84
Swastika Patch	120
Tree of Paradise	158
Triple Irish Chain	124
Triple Star	60
Tulip Quilt	46
Tumbling Blocks	150
Utility Quilt	26
W.P.A. Project Fan Quilt	154
Whig's Defeat	71
White House Appliqué Quilt	144
Whitework Quilt	98
Wool Comfort	130
Wool Nine-Patch	110
Yo-Yo Quilt	86

PROJECTS

Alabama Quilt Search Project	82, 186, 187
Arizona Quilt Project	104, 114, 121, 202, 203
Arkansas Quilter's Guild, Inc.	22, 146
Boise Basin Quilters Guild Registration Project	64, 158
California Heritage Quilt Project	180, 181, 196, 204
Colorado Quilting Council, Inc.	23, 76, 99
Columbia-Willamette Quilt Study Group	32, 33, 34
Connecticut Quilt Search Project	23, 84, 150
Delaware Folklife Project	172
Florida Quilt Heritage Project	36, 37, 116, 204
Georgia Quilt Project	23, 25, 44, 45, 96, 204
Hawaiian Quilt Research Project	42, 43, 126, 202
Heritage Quilt Project of New Jersey	122, 123, 179, 192, 193
Illinois Quilt Research Project	16, 23, 66, 130, 202
Indiana Quilt Registry Project	49, 81
Iowa Quilt Research Project	38, 92
Kansas Quilt Project	118, 119, 124
Kentucky Quilt Project, Inc.	15, 16, 108, 112, 174
Lancaster County Quilt Harvest	24, 48, 190, 191
Louisiana Quilt Search	19, 52, 134
"Made in DC" Quilt Search, Inc.	28, 170
Maryland Quilt Project	138, 195
MASS Quilts: The Massachusetts Quilt Documentation Project	68, 102
Michigan Quilt Project	80, 140, 204
Minnesota Quilt Project	110, 111, 156
Missouri Heritage Quilt Project	60, 198

Montana Heritage Quilt Project 23, 78
Nebraska Quilt Project 17, 18, 20, 178, 179
Nevada State Heritage Quilt Project 86
New Hampshire Quilt Documentation Project 98, 113
New York Quilt Project 23, 56, 142, 143
North Carolina Quilt Project . . .22, 25, 160, 182, 183, 203
North Dakota Quilt Project 30, 120, 121
Ohio Quilt Research Project 100, 175
Oklahoma Quilt Heritage Project 40, 41, 166
Oral Traditions Project .162, 163
Quilt Heritage: Washington State 22, 25, 74, 164, 204
Quilts of Tennessee 14, 176, 177, 181, 194
Rhode Island Quilt Documentation Project 136
South Carolina Quilt History Project 62, 71
Stitches in Time: A Legacy of Ozark Quilts 94, 106
Survey of the Hispanic Quiltmaking Tradition
   in Taos County 188
Texas Quilt Heritage Society 169
Texas Quilt Search 58
Utah Quilt Heritage Corporation 144
Vermont Quiltsearch 88, 132, 133
Virginia Quilt Research Project 46, 203
Virginia Search – Northern Virginia 128
West Virginia Heritage Quilt Search, Inc. 26, 184, 185

QUILTMAKERS

Abbott, Bertha and Lula 100, 101
Andres, Emma 104, 105
Austin, Harriet Beckett 26, 27
Baars, Inez Turner 164, 165
Beers, Mary A. 84, 85
Bender, Annie M. 172
Berry, Sarah 180, 181
Betit, Irene Fortier 132, 133
Black, Chany Scott 50, 51
Black, Narcissa L. Erwin .50, 51
Bland, Elsie Allred and
   the Help One Another Club 106, 107
Bomberger, Kathryn H. 190, 191
Bullock, Martha Jane Singleton Hatter 186, 187
Burris, Emma Hardin 71
Chesley, Melody Stolzfus with
   Pratt Museum Volunteers 200, 201
Clubb, Mary Jane 74, 75
Cobban, Mrs. Etta M. .148, 149
Cole, Drusilla Showalter 124, 125

Cooper, Narcissa Mayo .82, 83
Crabill, Elizabeth Jane Wymer 46
Craig, Josephine Hunter 118, 119
Cressy, Hannah M. 88, 89
Cushman, Elizabeth Diltz .112
David, Margaret (or Anna) .80
Deniston, Melissa Smith 158, 159
Diltz, Hanson Penn 112
Elgin, Carrie Diltz 112
Fisher, Marie 140, 141
Freeland, J. T. and Sarah Culbertson 81
Frick, Mrs. Charles (Estella Gwyn) 52, 53
Garrity, Margaret Fay 99
Girouard, Azelie Maillet 102, 103
Goff, Laurel Bangert 66, 67
Graves, Elizabeth Cope .60, 61
Gregg, Marina Jones 62, 63
Grigg, Helen 32, 33
Heim, Kate Smith Heslop 110, 111
Hicks, Eliza 92, 93
Hilliker, Myra P. 86, 87
Johnson, Phoeba 90, 91
Johnson, Victoria R. 54, 55
Kalama, Meali`i Namahoe Richardson 126, 127
Keefer, Cora Rute 162, 163
Kelley, Adele 126, 127
Kelley, Maria Namahoe 126, 127
Kenmore Quilters Patch of Kenmore, New York . . .142, 143
Kier, Bertha Granfor .120, 121
Ladies of Ebenezer Methodist
   Episcopal Church .170, 171
Larsen, Clara Louise Anderson 144, 145
Lloyd, Sarah Middleton 64, 65
Luce, Betsy Jane Young 56, 57
Lynch, Carolyn 128, 129
Lynes, Laura E. 198, 199
Manchester, Maria Fogg .113
Maxwell, Mary McCollough 94, 95
Mayer, Antoinette 28, 29
McClenny, Catherine Elizabeth (Kate) Waldron . . .116, 117
McCoy, Janet McCracken 175
McPhearson, Mrs. Green .146
Miller, Anna Hines (Mrs. Luther J.) 108, 109
Mission Band, Cedar Street Baptist Church . . .142, 143
Mitchell, Eugenia 76, 77
Moxley, Hetty Davis 34, 35
Nebraska Quilt Project Committee 18, 20

Pardee, Mary 152
Pawnee, Oklahoma High School
   Geometry Class of 1935 . . . . .40, 41
Pendroy, Sarah 30, 31
Peterson, Kjisti Erickson 164, 165
Phelan, Camille Nixdorf 166, 167
Poovey, Emma 160, 161
Powell, Elizabeth Ann Shipman 49
Pritchard, Allene Loveless 168, 169
Puyleart, Lucy 32, 33
Quigley, Jennie 134, 135
Ransbotham, Nellie L. Gates 150, 151
Richardson, Laura Violet 54, 55
Richardson, Mary Valeria 54, 55
Rockwell, Nona Thompson 184, 185
Sanchez, Elena Aguilar 188, 189
Saunders, Mrs. L. P. (Helen) 40
Shell, Minerva C. 194, 195
Shipley, Mary Linten .184, 185
Shuler, Ida Henderson .36, 37
Slaughter, Cora Viola Howell 114, 115
Smith, Anna Reed 130, 131
Smith, Frances Mooney 98
Smith, Sarah Elizabeth (Betty) Friddle 182, 183
Starksen, Anna Thoreson 156, 157
Sterns, Johanna (Hanna) Schmidt 78, 79
Stone, Hannah 38, 39
Stowe, Edith 114, 115
Stuart, Pomona Louvicy Forester 176, 177
Taber, Frank 68, 69, 70
Thrash, Lilla Owens 96, 97
Trueblood, Julia Ann Mills 58, 59
Volunteers of the Georgia Quilt Project 44, 45
W.P.A. Project 154, 155
Wellnitz, Martha (Mattie) Snowden Emerson 72, 73
White, Mary Elizabeth Lynes 196, 197
Willson, Sarah Clark .138, 139

QUILT OWNERS

Allen County Historical Society 100
Arizona Historical Society 114
Arkansas Territorial Restoration 146
Ashland Historic Society 98
Barnhart, Jane 102, 103
Basham, Juanita Austin Dove 26
Beaches Area Historical Society 116, 117

Name	Pages
Bennett, Ramona A.	164, 165
Best, Frankie	18
Betit, Hector T.	132, 133
Birky, Harold and Dorothy	38, 39
Bland, Ruth	106
Bomberger, Kathryn H.	190, 191
Brooks, Daniel	82
Buck, Mary Ann	156, 157
Buffalo and Erie County Historical Society	142, 143
Burleson, Vickie	182, 183
Cargo, Helen and Robert	186, 187
Carpenter, Dr. and Mrs. Paul R.	118
Carroll, Margaret Thurston	92
Charleston Museum	62
Charlet, Lynne	140, 141
Charlet, Mary Lee	140, 141
Cockrell, Mr. and Mrs. J. K. Jr.	170, 171
Cole, Bette G.	86, 87
Cornett, Kitty	194, 195
Crabill, Roger	46
Davis, Irma	58
Davis, Jacinta M.	124
Davis, Mary	96
De Angelis, Len	136, 137
Delaware Agricultural Museum and Village	152, 153
Dettner, Beth	56, 57
Doane, Rex and Phyllis	88, 89
Gaillour, Priscilla	188
Goff, Laurel Bangert	66, 67
Grigg, Helen	32, 33
Harris, Alice Lee	196, 197
Heavner, David C.	160, 161
Historical Society of Moorestown	122
Holcomb, Mrs. Edmund	150, 151
Hopp, Leota M.	58, 59
Hulst, Connie	120
Indiana State Museum	49, 81
Javernick, Charlene	64
Kane, Mrs. Howard N. (Dorothy J.)	68
Kelley, Clella Harris	40, 41
Kentucky Historical Society	112
Larsen, Reuben D.	144, 145
Leeper, Edith M.	60
Leonard, Mr. and Mrs. James	180, 181
Lincoln Quilters Guild	178, 179
Lynch, Carolyn	128, 129
Mayer, Steven	28
Michigan State University Museum	80
Miller, Edna Mae	78
Mississippi State Historical Museum	50, 51, 90
Montgomery County Historical Society	138, 139
Museum of Florida History	36, 37
Oklahoma State Museum of History	166
Park, Marguerite	30, 31
Peeler, Mrs. James M.	198
Pratt Museum	200, 201
Pritchard, Allene Loveless	168, 169
Razey, Arlie M.	74
Reno, Patricia	52
Reuben, Hilary Elizabeth	192, 193
Riedler, Elizabeth L.	144, 145
Rocky Mountain Quilt Museum	76, 77, 99
Ross County Historical Society, The	175
Ryska, Hazel	158, 159
Shelton, Martha Lou Boulton	176, 177
Slear, Gary and Donna	162
South Dakota State Historical Society	148, 149, 154
Stratford Historical Society	84
Sugg, Ollie	94, 95
Tetreau, Mark and Jill	104, 105
Wahlig, Mrs. Charles (Connie)	172
Walker, Clareta	130, 131
Wall, Mr. and Mrs. Allen	42
Weinraub, William C. L. (Bill)	44, 45
Weness, Jean	110, 111
Western Kentucky Museum	108
Whittington, Evelyn	64
Wyoming State Museum	54, 72
York County Historical Commission	71
Young, Isabella R.	184, 185
Zimmerman, Dorothy	34, 35

OTHER PERSONNEL

Name	Pages
Adams, Bryding	187
Ambrose, Sally	22
Akana, Elizabeth A.	127
Benberry, Cuesta	174
Best, Frankie	16, 17, 19, 179
Bibleheimer, Jane	191
Brackman, Barbara	39, 119
Christopherson, Katy	14, 16, 17
Clarke, Mary Washington	109
Clark, Ricky	16
Crews, Dr. Patricia	179
Downey, Lois	204
Dutton, Dr. William Rush, Jr.	15
Eller, Clyde	143
Emmons, Mary Ann	15
Finley, Ruth	119
Freeman, Roland	91
Hall, Carrie	105, 119, 167
Havig, Bettina	197
Hawley, Madelaine	22
Hecht, Rachel Baxter	183
Horton, Laurel	15, 63
Kennedy, Cheryl	16, 23, 202
Kretsinger, Rose	119, 167
Laury, Jean Ray	197
Lasansky, Jennette	163
Lenox, Barbara	24
Mann, Bruce	15, 148
Martinec, Jean Shuler	37
McElroy, Virginia	204
Miller, Eleanor Bingham	15
Mitchell, Eugenia Hartmeister	77, 99
Newman, Joyce Joines	15
Newman, Sharon	59
Peto, Florence	15
Pilgrim, Paul D.	14
Ramsey, Betts	14, 177
Reimer, Ann	179
Ronning, Kari	17, 19, 179
Roy, Gerald E.	14
Sears, Eunice	16
Tepper, Phyllis	48
Thompson, Phyllis`	48
Todaro, Sandra	19
Toney, Laura	25
Trechsel, Gail Andrews	177
Valentine, Fawn	185
Variable Star Quilters	155
Waite, Audrey	203
Waldvogel, Merikay	155, 177, 181
Weaver, Sandra	23
Webb, Elizabeth A. (Betsy)	200
Weinraub, Anita	25
Williams, Charlotte Allen	204
Winberg, Pam	45
Zegart, Shelly	15
Zopf, Dorothy	189

Museum of the American Quilter's Society
215 Jefferson St. / P. O. Box 1540
Paducah, KY 42002-1540
502-442-8856

OTHER MAQS EXHIBIT PUBLICATIONS

These books can be found in the MAQS bookshop and in local bookstores and quilt shops. If you are unable to locate a title in your area, you can order by mail from the publisher: AQS, P.O. Box 3290, Paducah, KY 42002-3290.

Please add $1 for the first book and $.40 for each additional one to cover postage and handling. International orders please add $1.50 for the first book and $1 for each additional one.

To order by VISA or MASTERCARD call: 1-800-626-5420 or fax: 1-502-898-8890.

Contemporary Quilts from The James Collection
Ardis James
#4525: AQS, 1995, 40 pages, 6" x 9", softbound, $12.95.

Nancy Crow: Quilts and Influences
Nancy Crow
#1981: AQS, 1990, 256 pages, 9" x 12", hardcover, $29.95.

Nancy Crow: Work in Transition
Nancy Crow
#3331: AQS, 1992, 32 pages, 9" x 10", softbound, $12.95.

New Jersey Quilts – 1777 to 1950: Contributions to an American Tradition
The Heritage Quilt Project of New Jersey
#3332: AQS, 1992, 256 pages, 8½" x 11", softbound, $29.95.

Quilts: Old and New, A Similar View
Paul D. Pilgrim and Gerald E. Roy
#3715: AQS, 1993, 40 pages, 8¾" x 8", softbound, $12.95.

Quilts: The Permanent Collection – MAQS
#2257: AQS, 1991, 100 pages, 10" x 6½", softbound, $9.95.

Quilts: The Permanent Collection, Volume II – MAQS
#3793: AQS, 1994, 80 pages, 10" x 6½", softbound, $9.95.

The Log Cabin Returns to Kentucky: Quilts from the Pilgrim/Roy Collection
Paul D. Pilgrim and Gerald E. Roy
#3329: AQS, 1992, 36 pages, 9" x 7", softbound, $12.95.

Victorian Quilts, 1875–1900: They Aren't All Crazy
Paul D. Pilgrim and Gerald E. Roy
#3932: AQS, 1994, 64 pages, 6" x 9", softbound, $14.95.